Credit Analysis

Walter S. Foster

TotalRecall Publications, Inc.
1103 Middlecreek
Friendswood, Texas 77546
281-992-3131 TEL
www.totalrecallpress.com

All rights reserved, except as permitted under the United States Copyright Act of 1976. No part of this publication may be reproduced, stored in a retrieval system, or transmitted in any form or by any means electronic or mechanical or by photocopying, recording, or otherwise, without prior permission of the publisher. Exclusive worldwide content publication/distribution by TotalRecall Publications, Inc.

Copyright © 2017 by: Walter S. Foster
All rights reserved

ISBN: 978-1-59095-971-8
UPC: 6-43977-39710-3

Printed in the United States of America with simultaneous printing in Australia, Canada, and United Kingdom.

FIRST EDITION
1 2 3 4 5 6 7 8 9 10

The scanning, uploading and distribution of this book via the internet or via any other means without the permission of the publisher is illegal and punishable by law. Please purchase only authorized electronic editions, and do not participate in or encourage electronic piracy of copyrighted materials. Your support of the author's rights is appreciated.

To all who trained and supported me through the years.

Corporate, Bank and Derivative Credit Risk Judgment

W. S. Foster Associates
Credit Development Specialists

W. S. Foster, President

Conducts seminars in Corporate and Bank Credit Risk Judgment.
Conducts seminars in Derivative Credit Risk Judgment and Management.
Conducts seminars in Credit Portfolio Risk Management
Conducts seminars in Evaluating Distressed Debt

<u>W. S. Foster Associates</u>
For over twenty years. W. S. Foster Associates has provided quality in-house training programs to a wide variety of U.S. and international institutions. The courses are for entry level as well as experienced investment bankers and financial professionals. W. S. Foster Associates' role as seminar leader has greatly enhanced the judgment and analytical skills of participants from hanks, investment hanks and rating agencies. Clients include:

Standard & Poor \s
Fannie Mae
National Australia Bank
Credit Suisse First Boston
Federal Reserve Bank of NY
Merrill Lynch
Bank of England

Jack Foster, primary instructor of W. S. Foster Associates, has unique qualifications to design and lead credit seminars. Over the past 20 years, he has conducted over 200 week long Corporate and Bank Credit Rating Seminars in over 15 countries including Saudi Arabia, Egypt, I long Kong, China, South Korea, Japan, Singapore, Indonesia, Australia, Mexico, Sweden, Switzerland, Germany, England, France, and the U.S. He started and was Chairman of the Rating Committee at JP Morgan for five years and served at JP Morgan for 20 years (1974-1994). He was the primary instructor for Standard and Poor's internal and external Bank and Corporate Credit analysis Seminars for eight years (1995-2003). He is a graduate of Williams College and the Harvard Business School.

WALTER S. (JACK) FOSTER

EMPLOYMENT

2002-2016 NEW YORK INSTITUTE OF FINANCE:
Conducted seminars in Corporate, Bank and Derivative Credit Risk Judgment in New York, Riyadh, Chicago and San Diego
Conducted seminars in Basel III and Systemically Important Financial Institutions
Developed electronic credit and corporate finance courses

Member RMA (Risk Management Association) CMCAS (Capital Markets Credit Analysts Society and, FIAS (Fixed Income Analysts Society).

1995-2002 STANDARD AND POOR'S:
Primary instructor for internal and external training programs. Conducted over 100 Corporate, Bank and Derivative Credit Risk week-long Seminars in 15 different countries.

1974-1994 JP MORGAN-
Credit Officer Global Markets '92-'94
Chairman, NACHO (North American Foreign Exchange Clearing House Organization)
Member, Executive Committee, ECHO (European Foreign Exchange Clearing House Organization)
Represented Global Markets' Credit in developing a single bank-wide credit system.
Rewrote and redesigned credit policy manual for bank-wide credit policy.
Designed and supervised implementation of computer tracking program for global sub-limits.
Credit Policy Department '83-'92
Chairman, North American Rating Committee -- rated all bank credit exposure.
Department Head, Risk Evaluation Group -- responsible for supervising 50 analysts.
Commercial Bank Management Program '82-'83
Administrator. Designed course content. Evaluated all trainees.
Financial Advisory Department '74-'82
Responsible for analytical work for internal ratings for manufacturing and basic industries.
Responsible for discontinuance of real estate lending in late 70's.

1967-1974 SELF EMPLOYED

1964-1967 CITICORP - ASSISTANT BRANCH MANAGER
Singapore, Kuala Lumpur

1959-1962 U.S. NAVY - LTJG
U.S. Naval Intelligence, Philippines

EDUCATION Masters Of Business Administration, Harvard University, 1964
1955-1964 Bachelor Of Arts, Williams College, 1959

PUBLICATIONS Co-authored <u>The Management of Racial Integration in Business</u> -- McGraw Hill 1964,
1964-2015 Authored <u>How to Avoid the Armageddon of 2054</u> -- Barringer Publishing 2015

W. S. Foster Associates Approach to Credit Development

W. S. Foster Associates (WSF) takes a different approach to credit training than is usually employed. Rather than just focus on the *instruction* of techniques and definitions such as cash flow measurement, financial statement analysis or accounting, or the *education* of credit analysis based on historic cases, WSF focuses on programs that create a future oriented credit *experience.* These programs develop a framework and methodology for evaluating credit risk using current 1OK/annual reports and industry information rather than historic cases. This framework and methodology leads to participant evaluation of future oriented credit ratings using current market concepts and information. And the ratings include outlooks that identify potential signs of deterioration and are expressed in terms of a percent likelihood of future default (company or issuer ratings) and percent likelihood of potential loss given default (facility or issue ratings).

The default rating methodology includes risk rating assessment of business risk (industry risk, competitive position, management) as well as financial risk (financial policy, profitability, leverage, cash flow and financial flexibility) as well as techniques for integrating these factors to come up with an overall default rating.

The loss rating methodology includes methods for evaluating recovery based on enterprise and liquidation values as well as on adjustments for collateral, covenants and structural and contractual seniority and subordination.

More important, while the training includes credit analysis, the primary focus is on credit judgment. Seminars use mock rating committees and group presentations as an aid to developing a working knowledge rather just a familiarity with the subject. Seminars include both investment grade and non-investment grade cases.

WSF uses public rating agency ratings of each aspect of credit risk as the standard for default ratings and public rating agency and bank expected loss methodologies as the standard for expected loss ratings. WSF then proceeds to discuss the strengths and weaknesses of the rating agency approach and how to make money by capitalizing on rating agency perceptions. WSF also provides methods for integrating default ratings and expected loss ratings on an overall risk equivalent basis and methodologies for using these ratings for pricing, reserving for losses, capital allocation and contributions to shareholder value.

Finally, WSF seminars evaluate this fundamentalist approach to credit ratings compared to market based and quantitative based credit risk rating systems.

The seminars involve pre-course reading material, course handout material, and post seminar methodologies for updating the material covered in the seminar.

New York Office - 641 Lexington Avenue, 15th Floor, New York, NY 10022, Tel. 212 756 8804

Table of Contents

Chapter 1: Introduction 1

Chapter 2: Rating Agency Credit Analysis (Business Risk) 14

    The Coca Cola Company Case 14

        Introduction 14

    Business Risk 17

        Industry Characteristics 17

        Parent/Subsidiary Links 21

Chapter 3: Rating Agency Credit Analysis (Financial Risk) 24

        Non-Investment Grade Credit 34

        Conclusion 35

    "Issue" Ratings ("Notching") 36

        Bank Loan Ratings and Evaluating Distressed Debt 37

        Sovereign Risk & Country Risk 41

Chapter 4: Regulatory Credit Analysis 46

        History of the Basel I and II Capital Accords 51

Chapter 5: Bank Credit Analysis 58

        Group Bank Rating Methodology 67

        Operational Risk Management 69

        Integrated Risk Management 70

        What Went Wrong? 72

Chapter: 6 Derivative Credit Analysis 73

    Exercise1: Questions Identifying Derivatives 76

    Exercise 1: Answers Identifying Derivatives 78

    Exercise 2: Questions Constructing Derivative Cash Flows 80

    Exercise 2: Answers: Constructing Derivative Cash Flows 82

Chapter 7: Conclusion 108

Chapter 1: Introduction

My name is Jack Foster. For five years, I was Chairman of the Credit Rating Committee at JP Morgan and was responsible for supervising all credit training. For seven years after JP Morgan, as a financial advisor, I was the primary instructor for credit analysis for Standard and Poor's (S&P). During that period, I taught over 100 week-long internal and external credit analysis courses for future S&P analysts and clients.

My approach to credit analysis and credit ratings is, therefore, based on these experiences and the examples I use are from my experience at JP Morgan and S&P.

A term often used today to describe institutional risk is "enterprise risk". Some analysts use enterprise risk because our increasingly complex financial world has increased the importance of other risk factors such as legal, operational, market and country risk. I have retained the term "credit risk" because I believe it better captures the fundamental importance of ethics in banking in particular and capitalism in general. I discuss this further in Chapter 7, Conclusion.

Development of Credit Analysis Skills:

We develop credit analysis skills in four stages. We can remember the four stages from the acronym DEEP - D for the Descriptive Stage, E for the Explanatory Stage, E for the Evaluative Stage and P for the Prescriptive Stage.

Descriptive Stage: The descriptive stage is about clarifying facts such as Company A is in the XYZ industry, its sales were $500 million and its net income was $50 million, etc.

Explanatory Stage: The explanatory stage provides reasons for the facts. Sales increased by 10% but only 7% was due to volume increases, the other 3% was due to price increases. Net income declined $5 million due to an extraordinary litigation charge. Debt declined $5 million due to a reduction in cash, etc.

Evaluative Stage: The evaluative stage integrates facts to clarify the most important factors that determine the credit rating. Debt to Earnings before Interest, Taxes,

Depreciation and Amortization (Debt to EBITDA ratio) decreased to 200%. Operating margins and net margins continued to increase at the same time sales and market share increased. The Company is planning large debt financed capital expenditures that we expect to increase Debt to EBITDA in the future, etc.

Prescriptive Stage: The prescriptive sage clarifies opportunities for extending credit or purchasing bonds. The plans for increased capital expenditures requires debt financing that we can help underwrite. We can help structure the financing so that the Company can maintain its credit rating. The bond offers an attractive yield for a BBB credit that has a positive outlook, etc.

While this book includes descriptive, explanatory and prescriptive aspects of credit analysis, it will primarily focus on the evaluative aspects. It will focus on how to evaluate the most important strengths and weakness of any company loan or bond.

Credit is the fuel of capitalism and is essential to a growing economy. Credit is the process of taking money from savers (who do not know how to invest) and lending it to financial intermediaries and borrowers who can invest the money in a way that contributes to economic growth.

The objective of this book is to clarify this process in its most simple terms. Therefore, the book will focus on the key factors, not the details of credit analysis. It will focus on the three to five-year evaluation of bond and loan credit risk, not short-term credit risk or market risk.

The most important aspects of credit analysis is objectivity and integrity - a methodical and honest evaluation of the facts. This may seem obvious but the experiences of the recession of 2008/2009 demonstrates that it is easy for many bankers, investment bankers and borrowers to put their short-term economic benefits ahead of long-term interests of their clients and their long-term ability to repay debt. (See Chapter 7, Conclusion.)

The aim will be to demonstrate how economics and politics, capitalism and democracy, competence and fairness, ethics and morality and our political party system affect credit analysis. In other words, the aim will be to demonstrate how credit analysis fits in as a part of the all the other factors in our life.

In credit analysis, we have three levels of certainty - facts we can know beyond all doubt, decisions we can make beyond a reasonable doubt and decisions we can make based upon the preponderance of evidence. For example, in legal analysis for civil cases, we only need to demonstrate our case by a preponderance of evidence. In legal analysis for criminal cases, we need to demonstrate our case beyond a reasonable doubt. In scientific proofs, we need to demonstrate our case beyond all doubt. In credit analysis some things we know beyond all doubt - for example accounting rules; some things we know beyond a reasonable doubt - for example financial statement analysis, and cash flow analysis; and finally some things we only know based upon the preponderance of evidence — for example credit analysis and credit understanding. Credit analysis is an art not a science, it comes up with probabilities for decision making under conditions of uncertainty.

The question is "How do we evaluate those conditions of uncertainty?" The generally accepted standard for evaluating individual credits is the methodology used by the rating agencies. The recession of 2008/2009, however, raised questions about this methodology.

Therefore, it is first necessary to review what went wrong with the rating agency methodology in 2008/2009 to identify its limitations. After clarifying these limitations, we can then use the rating agency methodology as the standard for evaluating credit from the perspective of an individual loan or security. We will then look at how the regulators look at evaluating credit risk in the banking system from the perspective of U.S taxpayers. Next, we will look at how banks evaluate their own credit risk across a portfolio of loans from the perspective of shareholders. Finally, we will look at how to evaluate derivative credit risk from the perspective of derivative traders and bank management.

The objective of this review is to integrate credit risk standards from different perspectives as a means of clarifying analytical techniques and increasing critical thinking.

The first way to evaluate credit risk is from the perspective of the probability of default. The second is from the probability of loss.

Risk of Default - PD or Probability of Default: Default is the failure of timely payment of principal and interest and we express the likelihood of that default in percentage terms. For example, the percent likelihood of default for a BBB credit over 1 year, 5 years, 10,years, etc.

Risk of Loss - LGD or Loss Given Default: Loss is the difference between the face value of a loan or security relative to principal and interest received discounted back to the date of default. For example, the percent likelihood of loss for a BB credit once a default has occurred.

The two perspectives result in two different types of ratings. The first type of rating is the issuer rating from the perspective of the probability of default. The second type or rating is the issue rating from the perspective of the probability of default and the expected loss given default.

Issuer Ratings - Default Risk Ratings of Corporates, Counterparties and Sovereigns: Rating agencies base issuer ratings on the capacity and willingness of borrowers to meet financial commitments on time.

Issue Rating — Loss Risk Ratings of specific financial obligations: Rating agencies base issue ratings on the default risk rating but also include an assessment of the ultimate recovery prospects after default due to seniority in the capital structure, guarantees, collateral, covenants etc.

Rating agency ratings also include two additional ratings - Outlook Ratings and Credit Watch Ratings.

Outlook Ratings: Rating Agencies assign Outlook Ratings to all long-term issuer ratings. They assess the potential long-term direction of the rating over a time horizon of up to 3 years. They are not necessarily a precursor to a rating change. The four types of outlook ratings are Positive, Negative, Stable and Developing.

Credit Watch Ratings: Rating Agencies assign Credit Watch Ratings selectively to long-term Issuer Ratings. They focus on the short-term direction of the company due to changes in fundamentals or significant events such as a large acquisition. The time horizon is usually 90 days or less while the Rating Agency is able to obtain the additional information necessary to complete the rating process. There are three types of Credit Watch Ratings - Positive, Negative and Developing.

The rating scale for both long-term Issuer and Issue ratings for S&P runs from AAA to D.

Rating Agency Short-Term Ratings: In addition to long-term Issuer and Issue ratings the rating agencies also rate short-term debt with a maturity of one-year or less such as commercial paper or certificates of deposit. The four categories of short-term ratings for S&P are A-1+, A-l, A-2, A-3 and B. A company's short-term ratings is largely determined by its long-term rating. For example, a company with a long term S&P rating of AAA to A+ receives an A-1+ short term rating, A+ to A- an A-1 short-term rating, an A+ to BBB an A-2 rating, a BBB to BBB- an A-3 rating and a BB+ to BB- a B short term rating. Whenever there are overlaps, S&P gives the higher or lower rating depending upon the Company's liquidity, i.e. its amount of cash, committed credit facilities etc. Rating Agency Ratings are relevant to banks and investors because they provide a short cut for less sophisticated investors to choose more or less credit risk and implicitly, more or less market volatility. Historically, higher quality investment grade companies rated BBB- or better have had substantially less frequent rating changes, market volatility and loss than lower quality non-investment grade credits rated BB+ or lower.

Rating Agency ratings are highly respected. Their ratings have historically been viewed as independent (the Rating Agencies are paid a fixed fee and have nothing to gain from whether their rating is higher or lower). There has been a close correlation between ratings and default and the Rating Agencies have been transparent about their rating criteria.

However, the recession of 2008/2009 revealed weaknesses in the methodology for rating mortgage backed structured finance transactions. Like almost everyone else, the rating agencies underestimated the cyclicality of real estate. In 2008, their historical ability to predict defaults of corporate obligors over the previous 30 years had been extremely accurate over any time-period. Over one-year the approximate average annual default rate for S&P was 0.0% for AAA rated credits, 0.2% for BBB rated credits and 26.4% for CCC rated credits. Over 5 years the average cumulative default rate for S&P was 0.4% for AAA rated credits, 2.0% for BBB rated credits and 46.3% for CCC rated credits. Even over 10 years the average cumulative default rate for S&P was approximately 0.7% for AAA rated credits, 4.0% for BBB rated credits and 50.7% for CCC rated credits.

S&P Corporate Default Risk by Rating*
Average <u>Cumulative</u> Default Rates 1981-2015 (%)

Year#	**AAA**	AA	A	**BBB**	BB	B	**CCC/C**
1	**0.00**	0.02	0.07	**0.20**	0.76	3.88	**26.38**
2	0.03	0.07	0.16	0.57	2.35	8.80	35.58
3	0.14	0.13	0.27	0.98	4.23	12.97	40.67
4	0.24	0.24	0.41	1.46	6.06	16.22	43.77
5	**0.36**	0.35	0.57	**1.95**	7.71	18.70	**46.28**
10	**0.74**	0.82	1.51	**4.06**	13.74	25.91	**50.73**
15	0.98	1.19	2.32	5.84	16.77	29.49	53.38

*S&P Annual Corporate Default Study 2015, Table 24

In other words, if S&P rates a credit AAA, the one-year possibility of default should be should be less than one-in-a-thousand i.e. the financial markets expect the borrower to pay interest and principle on time 99.9% of the time, i.e. beyond all doubt. If S&P rates a credit BBB the one-year possibility of default should be about one-in-500 i.e. the financial markets expect the borrower to pay interest and principle on time 99.8% of the time i.e. within a reasonable doubt. If S&P rates a credit, C the one-year possibility of default should be about one-in-two i.e. the financial markets expect that the borrower will repay interest and principle on time 50% of the time i.e. there is an even chance that the borrower will repay interest and principle on time. In fact, in the previous 34 years there has been only one large "corporate" that has been rated investment grade i.e. BBB- or higher at the time of default and that was Lehman Brothers.

Largest Corporate Defaults*
(2001-2015, US$ Billions)

	Amt.	Year	Rating**
Lehman Brothers Holdings Inc.	$144	2008	A
Ford Motor Company	$ 71	2009	CC
General Motors Corporation	$ 53	2009	CC
GMAC LLC	$ 46	2008	CC
Energy Future Holdings	$ 48	2010	CC
WorldCom Inc.	$ 34	2002	B
Texas Competitive Electric Holds	$ 32	2011	B-
Lyondell Basell Industries (Dutch)	$ 24	2008	B-
Harrah's Entertainment Inc.	$ 24	2008	CC
Chrysler	$ 23	2009	CC

* Includes Distressed Exchanges

** At time of default

It is not hard to see from this table what a shock it was to the financial markets for the Federal Reserve to allow Lehman Brothers to go into default. As a result of this event and other factors:

- The interbank market was frozen and the Fed had to replace that market with its discount window. (The discount window permits banks to provide investment grade loans as collateral and receive cash from the Federal Reserve in return.)

- The largest 19 banks had to accept equity infusions from the Troubled Asset Relief Program. (It was later estimated by a congressional committee that only one of those 19 banks (JP Morgan) would have survived without the Troubled Asset Relief Program).

- The commercial paper and money fund markets were frozen and, in effect, the Fed had to guarantee them.

- The Department of the Treasury and the Fed put Fannie Mae and Freddie Mac into conservatorship and began purchasing a large portion of their securities.

People began blaming other people for the crisis.

- *"The problem was not a lack of regulation, but firms' poor judgment."* Alan Greenspan, former Chairman of the Federal Reserve to the Financial Crisis Inquiry Commission. April 7, 2010.
- "The incessant broad based vilification of the banking industry isn't fair and it is damaging. Punishing whole industries, whether you were reckless or not, just isn't the way to do things." *James Dimon, Chairman and Chief Executive of J. P. Morgan Chase & Co. Wall Street Journal April 7, 2010.*
- "Letter to shareholders increases from 4 pages in 2008 to 9 pages in 2009 justifying activities during crisis." *Lloyd Blanfein, Chief Executive Officer, Goldman Sachs.*

In fact, everyone was to blame for the crisis. The crisis was a one in a hundred years event. To use the highway analogy, "Everyone was driving too fast for conditions." Government, Business, Consumers. Some people were driving faster than others, but all traffic was moving too fast, i.e., there was too much leverage, too much optimism, too loose credit standards. "Buy the largest house you can possibly afford and it will appreciate in value." Everyone was living off the <u>asset inflation bonus</u>. An asset inflation bonus makes everyone feel wealthier because their homes, stocks, bonds, etc. are worth more.

Corporate credit quality had been declining for years. On average, from 1984 to 2004, S&P downgraded many more companies each year compared to the number of corporates they upgraded.

The Long Term Decline in Corporate Credit Quality
Downgrade-to-Upgrade Ratio Global 1981-2015
S&P 2015 Annual Corporate Default Study Table 6
Downgrades/Upgrades

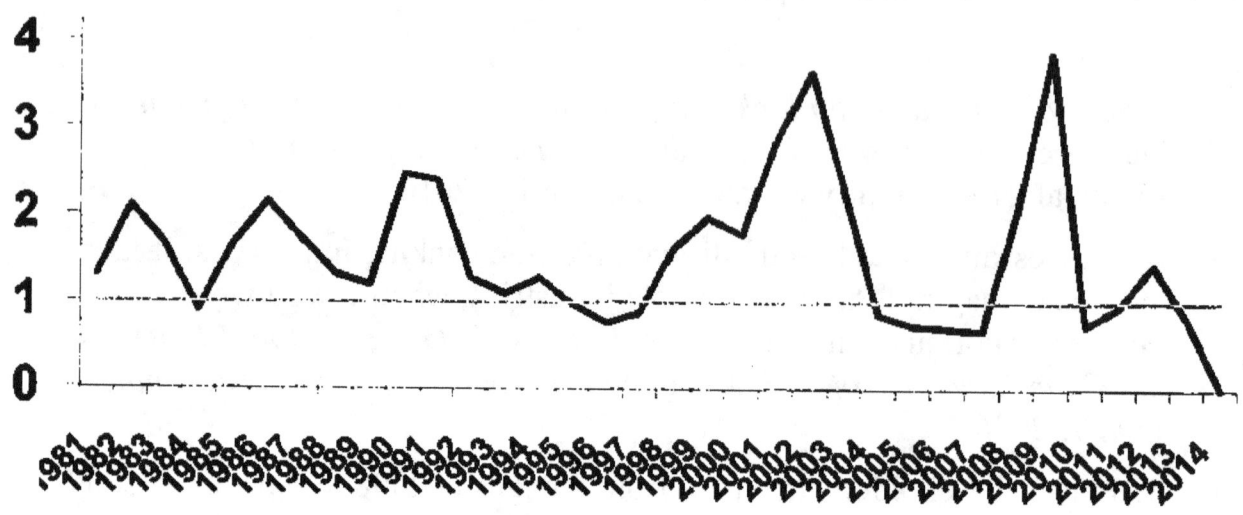

Household Sector Net Assets
(Current $ in Trillions)

2003	$46	
2004	$52	
2005	$58	
2006	$62	
2007	$67	(Inflation Adjusted -- $84 in 2015 dollars)*
2008	$56	
2009	$58	
2010	$62	
2011	$63	
2012	$70	
2013	$80	
2014	$84	
2015	$87	

There was a deflation in Household Sector wealth. Household Sector Net Assets declined 16% in 2008.

In 2008, approximately $28 Trillion of Household Total Net Assets were in homes compared to mortgage debt of $10 trillion.

	Trillions
• Household Total Income (GDP)	$10
• Household Total Net Assets	$28
• Household Mortgages debt	$14
• Total Net Assets in homes	$56

In 2008 GDP was $ 14 trillion versus total asset values of $56 trillion i.e. asset values were very high relative to cash flow (GDP). *The important point to remember, however, is that a systemic crisis hurts everyone.*

	Losses in $ billions
• The Consumer (Decline in Net Asset Value)	$12,000
• The Economy (2009 Reduced GDP)	$ 500
• The Government (2009 Deficit)	$ 1,500
• Goldman Sachs 2009 Net Income	$ 13
• Goldman Sachs Increased Taxes	$?
• Goldman Sachs Increased Regulatory Restrictions	$?
• Goldman Sachs Pensions, Houses etc.	$?

The question is how do we effectively evaluate credit after learning the lessons from the 2008/2009 crisis? How can we make the next panic less severe? In order to understand how to make the next panic less severe it is necessary to understand the myths that caused the 2008 liquidity panic. Only by understanding these myths can we better understand how to evaluate credit and the reasons for the recent regulatory changes.

There were three myths that caused the crisis of September 2008.

- Real estate loans are like any other loans. (80% of the cause).
- Credit derivatives are like any other derivatives. (10% of the cause).
- Developed market based economies do not need regulation. (10% of the cause.

Myth #1 - 80% of the Cause: Real estate loans are like any other loans:

Banks, regulators, rating agencies—everyone assumed real estate loans were like other loans. In 2008, this was clearly not the case. Real estate is a far more cyclical industry than other industries. According to the Kondratieff Theory, once in every 100 years asset values become out of line with income. Asset values to income builds up gradually over many years but the excess only becomes apparent over a short period after a rapid rise in real estate prices. One hundred years is a difficult period for business decision making. The result was that in 2008 there were declines in real estate values of approximately 30%. Because there were almost $10 trillion in residential mortgage loans outstanding in 2008, the financial markets expected the losses from mortgage lending to be so great there was a question as to whether or not the banks could absorb the losses. In addition, the rating agencies had rated over 15,000 securitized residential mortgage back securities.

S&P had stated in their *Structured Finance Criteria* "Our ratings represent a uniform measure of credit quality globally across all types of debt instruments. In other words, an AAA-rated corporate bond should exhibit the same degree of credit quality as an AAA rated securitized debt issue." In the past, S&P on average downgraded AAA corporate securities to non-investment grade in one year less than **.1%** of the time.

S&P Normal Global Corporate Average One-Year Transition Rates

	RATING AT YEAR-END %							
	AAA	AA	A	BBB	BB	B	CCC	D
AAA	87.1	9.0	0.5	0.1	**0.1**	**0.0**	**0.0**	**0.00**
AA	0.5	86.7	8.1	0.5	0.1	0.0	0.0	0.0
A	0.03	1.8	87.7	5.4	0.3	0.1	0.0	0.0
BBB	0.0	0.1	3.6	85.4	3.8	0.5	0.1	0.2
BB	0.0	0.0	0.1	5.1	76.8	7.0	0.6	0.76
B	0.0	0.0	0.1	0.2	5.3	74.3	4.4	3,8
CCC	0.0	0.0	0.1	0.2	0.6	12.8	44.92	26.4

In 2008-2009, the rating agencies downgraded over 22% of the 15,000 AAA residential mortgage structured finance ratings to non-investment grade compared to only 3% of the 160 corporate AAA ratings.

Accuracy of S&P Ratings 2008-2009 Combined

<u>Corporate</u> AAA Ratings at Year-end
% Downgraded to Non-investment Grade *
(2% of All Ratings Were AAA - (Starting Total AAAs - <u>120</u>)

	BB	B	CCC*	D	Total
2008-2009 AAAs	0.06	1.01	2.02	**0.00**	**3.09**
Normal AAAs	0.16	0.06	0.12	**0.00**	**0.34**

<u>Structured Finance</u> AAA Ratings at Year-end
% Downgraded to Non-investment Grade *
(20% of All Ratings Were AAA - (Starting Total AAAs - <u>15.464</u>)

	BB	B	CCC	D	Total
2008-2009 AAAs	4.94	7.10	10.05	**0.86**	**22.95**
Normal AAAs	0.16	0.06	0.12	**0.00**	**0.34**

*2008-9 S&P Global Corporate and Structured Finance Default Studies. Studies Include total of 5,966 Corporate Ratings and 77,319 Structured Finance Ratings

The result was a loss of confidence in the ability of the rating agencies to assess credit risk.

The effects on the commercial banks were equally great because they had internally rated their own mortgage loans very highly as well. Their portfolio risk management methodology used internal credit ratings and transition risk as a method for allocating capital. They allocated almost no capital for their internally rated AAA mortgage loans based upon historic transitions of AAAs. Most commercial banks only reported their losses gradually as they increased their loan loss reserves each quarter. Investment banks, however, had large trading inventories of AAA rated structured finance securities that declined in market value immediately. These securities had to be marked-to-market daily and the resulting losses had to be run through their income statement immediately.

In summary, the failure of the real estate markets caused:

- *Ratings:* A loss of confidence in the rating system.
- *Bank losses:* Substantial write-downs of securitized mortgage loans and securities for investment banks, even when the loans were not in default or close to default due to declines in market values.

- *Changes in Rating criteria:* The Rating Agencies changed their rating methodology for U.S. residential mortgage-backed securities (RMBS) using the U.S. Great Depression of the 1930s as the AAA downside case rather than milder more current recessions.

Myth #2 -10% of the Cause: Credit derivatives are like other derivatives.

Credit derivatives are not like other derivatives. Foreign exchange rates and interest rates follow a normal volatility distribution with values changing daily. Credit default swaps variability follows an abnormal distribution since recessions cause values to change only every few years. Exchange rates and interest rates are liquid markets. Credit default swaps are like insurance contracts, not derivatives. Credit default swaps losses are catastrophic losses like hurricanes and vary widely from year to year. Therefore, like insurance contracts, in a financial crisis, credit derivatives are illiquid. During recessions, the market collapses. Nonetheless, in 2008-2009 for capital purposes, credit derivatives only had to be capitalized based on their one-year market volatility while their illiquidity and real volatility only occurred once every several years during recessions or financial crises. As a result, credit derivatives aggravated the effects of the Lehman bankruptcy on the market and required the Fed to bail out AIG.

Myth #3 -10% of the Cause: Developed Market-based Economies Don't Need Regulation:

Market economies are democratic economies. Just like political democracy, economic democracy needs checks and balances i.e. government regulation. Possible government regulation that might have reduced the severity of the 2008- 2009 recession include a bank-sponsored Derivative Clearing House that would have permitted the government to use its efforts to support the Clearing House rather than having to support individual institutions like Bear Stems & AIG. Similarly, regulations requiring banks to retain on their balance sheet a portion of securitized transactions might have caused bankers to be more cautious and reduced the magnitude of the deterioration in credit quality in real estate loans.

On the other hand, when the crisis came the Federal Reserve, the Secretary of the Treasury and Congress did a fantastic job of avoiding our spiraling into a depression. In spite of extensive popular opposition, the Congress passed the Dodd-Frank Act with the support of Senator Dodd and Congressman Frank who did not even try to be re-elected because of public opposition to their efforts.

In summary, the liquidity panic of 2008 was a once in a lifetime event. However, the ramifications of this event have released forces that affect the way to evaluate credit in the future. Living with an *asset deflation tax* has resulted in very low interest rates and pressure on consumer income from debt repayment and higher credit standards. It has resulted in high levels of discontent. Consumers and banks have faced a constant struggle to *de-leverage* through debt write-offs, debt repayment and/or reduced new borrowing.

The Federal Reserve has been afraid to raise interest rates for fear of causing more deflation or a recession. The result has been that recapitalization efforts have been insufficient to evaluate levels of credit worthiness to satisfy regulators. As a result, there has been a return to credit fundamentals—operating cash flow and liquidity and less reliance on asset values.

Now that we are past the crisis, the danger of the 2008-2009 recession is that new regulations will become overly restrictive. The Main Street view is that credit derivatives and selling short are to a free economy what yelling fire in a crowded theater is to free speech. The Main Street view is that the Fed bailed out the banks, but no one bailed out the consumer. The challenge is to balance new regulation with creativity and flexibility in a hostile political environment. The challenge is for rating agencies and banks is to regain credibility through more responsible and ethical lending and practices. In fact, because of changed regulations banks have been hurt, not just Main Street. Stock prices for most banks were still below what they were a decade ago until recently.

Chapter 2:
Rating Agency Credit Analysis (Business Risk)

Rating agencies use four stages to evaluate Corporate Credit Ratings. The first stage is Country Risk, the second is Business Risk, the third is Financial Risk and the fourth is Issue Risk.

We will discuss Country and Issue risk later in Chapter 3. Instead, we will start by reviewing the second and third stages i.e. Business Risk and Financial Risk. Business Risk analysis evaluates industry characteristics, competitive position, and management. Financial Risk analysis evaluates financial policy, profitability, capital structure, cash flow protection, and financial flexibility/liquidity.

We will use the Coca Cola Company as the case for Corporate Credit Risk. The reason we use Coke as the corporate credit risk company is that the carbonated soft drink industry is an industry that everyone understands. In addition, Coke provides outstanding financial information.

The Coca Cola Company Case
Introduction

The Coca Cola Company ("Coke") is the largest manufacturer, distributor and marketer of non-alcoholic beverage concentrates and syrups in the world. Coke sells over 500 different finished beverage products bearing its trademarks in over 200 countries. Coke's has a market leadership in carbonated soft drinks with a dominant market share of more than 50% worldwide and 40% in the United States. Of the approximately 58 billion beverage servings of all types consumed worldwide every day, beverages bearing the trademark owned by or licensed to Coke account for more than 3.0% or 1.9 billion. Carbonated beverages represent approximately 73% of worldwide unit case volume. Beverages with the Coca Cola name (Coca Cola, Diet Coca Cola, etc.) account for 46% of worldwide unit case volume.

Coke's largest competitor in carbonated soft drinks is Pepsi with an approximately 31% U.S. domestic market share. In 2015, Coke's unit case growth, consisting primarily of carbonated soft *drinks, but also including other beverage products, was 2% on a consolidated basis worldwide. Nineteen percent of sales came from the United States and 81% outside the United States. In 2015, Net Operating Revenues were $44.3 billion, Net Income was $7.4 billion and Assets were $90 billion. $33 billion of Coke's assets were current assets and $57 billion of Coke's assets were fixed assets. Of the $57 billion in fixed assets $12 billion were equity method investments in minority owned bottlers, $12 billion were property, plant and equipment, and $23 billion were trademarks, bottlers franchise rights and good will.*

Coke's business strategy is to use its assets including:

- *Its brands,*
- *Its financial strength,*
- *Its unrivalled distribution strength,*
- *Its global reach, and*
- *Its strong commitment of management and employees,*

to become more dominant and to accelerate growth in a manner that creates value for its shareholders. Moreover, Coke has undertaken a number of initiatives over the years with its bottlers, who play an important role in Coke's overall business plan.

Bottler Investment Strategy:

Bottling operators of Coke are entities that possess exclusive licenses to bottle and distribute Coke products within specified regions. In the United States, these exclusive distribution licenses are perpetual. The licenses do not allow anyone else to distribute Coca-Cola products in their franchise area. There are three types of bottlers that comprise the Coke system: (1) bottlers who are independently owned, and in which Coke has no ownership interest (34% by volume), (2) bottlers in which Coke has a non-controlling, minority ownership (38% by volume), and, (3) bottlers in which Coke owns a controlling interest (18% by volume). (The remaining 10% by volume consists of fountain sales directly by Coke.) Among many of the independent and non-controlled bottlers, owners are typically family investors who, in addition to contributing to management of the bottling operation, have significant portions of their wealth tied up in the bottling entity.

Historically, Coke granted exclusive distribution rights to a bottler in order to induce the bottler to make the substantial capital expenditures necessary for bottling operations. More recently, Coke has acquired an interest in its bottlers to ensure long-term strategic alignment with its more substantial bottlers. In some instances, Coke purchases controlling interests in bottlers, often to facilitate operational and/or financial improvements, and then sells its interest to one of the equity method bottler/investees.

Coke's ongoing minority ownership interests generally range between 15% and 49%, although there is no specific formula for the size of its investment, which can change over time. Some investments involve Coke board representation, and, through Coca-Cola Financial Corp., Coke may provide financing to some of its bottlers. Bottler investments provide Coke with increased concentrate sales, annual equity income, and the realization of a gain (or loss) when Coca Cola reduces or sells the investment. This method of investment also allows Coke to maximize the cash flow and value of its concentrate business. At yearend 2015, Coke had substantial equity positions in about 52 unconsolidated bottlers worldwide. These investments, accounted for by the equity and cost methods, totaled $12.3 billion in 2014 and represented approximately 14% of total assets. (If valued at the December 31, 2015 quoted closing prices of shares actively traded on stock markets, the value of the equity method investments in publicly traded bottlers would have exceeded the carrying value by $7.2 billion.) In addition, intangibles consisting of goodwill, bottler franchise rights and trademarks with indefinite lives, totaled $22.3 billion or 25% of total assets.

The level of Coke equity investment in its worldwide bottling system has increased over recent years, through which Coke has sought to increase its international penetration through acquisitions while also facilitating bottler consolidation within the domestic market. Much of this acquisition activity has been debt financed at the bottler level. Most of the bottler level debt does not have legal recourse to Coke (i.e. is not guaranteed by The Coca-Cola Company.) Coke has designated certain important affiliates as key bottlers. S&P characterizes key bottlers by their large size, geographical diversification and financial and managerial resources. Key bottlers are strongly committed to Coke's strategic plans, and have typically been Coke's primary vehicles for international expansion and domestic bottler consolidation.

Until 2010, key bottlers and other equity investees accounted for around 67% of Coke's worldwide volume. In 2010, Coca Cola acquired Coca Cola Enterprises' North America bottling operations that accounted for 88% of U.S. unit case volume. Coca Cola's 2016 strategic plan calls for refranchising these bottling operations by the end of 2017 and reducing company owned bottling operations from 18% to 3% of worldwide volume. Currently, Cokes other key bottlers span broad geographic areas and include CCHBC, CCA, Coca Cola FEMSA, Pan- American Beverages, Swire Pacific, and others. Under most bottler agreements, Coke has complete flexibility to determine the price and other terms of sale of the concentrates and syrups it sells.

Questions for Review and Discussion:

1. What are Coke's key drivers for success in the marketplace?
2. What are the key factors that set Coke apart from its competitors?
3. How would you evaluate Coke's opportunities for growth?
4. What are the key drivers of Coke's financial policies?
5. How would you describe Coke's financial performance?
6. What is the nature of the relationship between Coke and its bottlers, and is the relationship the same with all bottlers?
7. How does the rating of Coke influence the rating of its bottlers?
8. How does the rating of its bottlers influence the rating of Coke?
9. What criteria would you suggest as important in the evaluations of parent and subsidiary/affiliate relationships?

Readers can obtain more detailed information in Coca Cola's Annual Review and 10K located at CocaCola.com - Investor Relations -- Financial Information.

Business Risk

Business risk consists of industry characteristics, competitive position and management.

Industry Characteristics

Industry characteristics consist of industry structure, market size, growth potential, basis of competition, cyclicality, investment requirements & asset structure, rate of technological change, operating risk and regulatory environment.

Industry Structure: Rating agencies evaluate industry structure by whether it produces stable and predictable cash flow. They evaluate industry structure by whether the industry is fragmented or concentrated, easy to enter, local, national or global and limited or unlimited capacity.

The carbonated soft drink industry is attractive from a creditor's perspective because it is a concentrated industry with the top two companies Coca Cola and Pepsi controlling approximately 71% of the U.S. and worldwide market. Normally, being a concentrated industry reduces risk because there are fewer competitors. As a branded consumer product industry, the industry is difficult to enter - a good thing from a competitive point of view.

Coca Cola has been in business developing its brand for over 100 years and Pepsi for over 70 years. Both Coca Cola and Pepsi are highly diversified geographically, which diversifies country risk. Coca cola for example sells in over 200 countries. As a low fixed cost industry, there are no capacity (supply and demand) problems. If Coke or Pepsi produce too many bottles of soft drink one day, they merely slow down the bottling operation the next day with little effect on their profitability. (On the other hand, in a heavily fixed cost industry like the cement industry, if demand declines companies still have large fixed costs to absorb encouraging participants to reduce price to the point where they are at least covering variable costs.)

Market size: Rating agencies measure market size in terms of revenue and unit volume. An industry with large revenues and unit volumes is generally more attractive from a creditor's point of view since there are greater opportunities for economies of scale and the resources to attract professional managements.

In 2015, Coca Cola alone had $44 billion in annual revenues and therefore the carbonated soft drink industry is attractive because it is large enough to attract professional management and obtain large economics of scale.

Growth potential: Rating agencies measure growth both in relative and absolute terms. Growth slower than competitors i.e. declining market share is a negative while growth faster than competitor i.e. increasing market share is a positive. Modest growth generally reduces a company's credit risk. Companies that are growing rapidly can have problems successfully managing the growth. Companies with negative growth face the danger of substantial off-balance sheet and management costs such as severance payments, plant closures and a demoralized work force. Global carbonated soft drink growth is flat to moderate and therefore relatively easy to manage.

Basis of Competition: The most common basis of competition consists of:

- *Price* such as in the pulp & paper and commodity chemicals industries;
- *Quality* such as in the aircraft manufacturing industry;
- *Product differentiation* such as in the automobile industry;
- *Service* such as in the cable television industry;
- *Image* such as in the branded consumer products industry;
- *Technology* such as in the software and computer components industries; and
- *Regulatory* such as in the telecoms, utilities and banking industries

Coca Cola and Pepsi are in the Branded Consumer Products Industry, an attractive industry from a creditor's point of view since it produces stable and predictable cash flows.

Industry Cyclicality: Non-cyclical industries are more attractive than cyclical industries since there is an implied predictability in cash flows. In cyclical industries, rating agencies try to rate through the cycle i.e. expecting above average performance for a given rating during boom periods and below average performance during recessions. The difficulty of cyclical companies, however, is being able to discern whether the underperformance is due to a normal economic cycle or an indication of a secular decline. Most fixed asset intensive industries tend to be cyclical. They tend to have relatively low sales to total assets and relatively high fixed assets to total assets.

The carbonated soft drink industry is unusual in that at first glance it appears to have relatively low sales to assets (Coke's ratio is .5/1.0 compared to the average light manufacturer of 1.8/1.0) and relatively high fixed assets to total assets (Coke's ratio is .5/1 versus .2/1.0 for the average light manufacturer.) The reason for this is the goodwill created by Coke's purchase accounting acquisitions of their formerly independent bottlers. Only a relatively small portion of its assets is property, plant and equipment. Even though it is in what appears to be a less attractive fixed cost industry, the carbonated soft drink industry is an attractive industry because participants are able to obtain very high returns on capital (more than 20%) suggesting that the good will, franchise rights and other intangibles are undervalued.

Investment Requirements and Asset Structure: Investment requirements consists of working capital, property, plant, equipment and research & development.

Industries with large working capital requirements tend to be more attractive than industries with large plant and equipment and research and development because profits tend to increase at the same time there is increased need for working capital. Plant, equipment and research and development requirements tend to be more cyclical and less predictable.

One of the reasons that Coke and Pepsi are attractive from a creditor's point of view is because they have low working capital, property, plant, equipment and research and development requirements.

Technological Change: The rate of technological change increases vulnerability to becoming outdated. Industries with rapid rates of technological change tend to have less predictable cash flows. On the other hand, industries with modest technological change tend to have the opportunity to gradually reduce their cost of goods sold.

Coke and Pepsi are attractive because they have modest technological change in their industry. As a result, they have continually been able to reduce their costs of producing and distributing soft drinks about 6% a year due to gradual technological improvements in bottling equipment and efficiencies in distribution.

Factors of Production: Factors of production consist of inputs such as supply and cost of raw materials. Coke and Pepsi have no problems obtaining the ingredients to their soft drinks that consist mainly of sugar, water, artificial sweeteners and aluminum for cans and plastic and glass for bottles.

Operating Risk: Operating risk consists of risks of catastrophes like the Exxon Valdez, BP or Bhopal disasters. The largest operating risk in the soft drink bottling industry is contamination of the product. Even when Coke and Pepsi have had problems (a customer found a dead mouse in one bottle of Coca Cola), the adverse effects have been mild and short lived.

Regulatory Environment: Regulatory risks consists of potential adverse changes in regulations. Regulatory risk is occurring in the carbonated soft drink industry through attempts to reduce obesity and litter. However, to date, these regulations have occurred only gradually and have been manageable. Coke and Pepsi have reduced their exposure to obesity regulation by expansion into other, healthy beverages such as fruit juice and water.

Industries with excellent industry characteristics include global pharmaceuticals, branded consumer products and publishing. Industries with vulnerable industry characteristics include tires, integrated steel, construction and telecom.

Competitive Positon

Competitive position consists of market positon, cost positon and management.

Market position: Market position consists of market share, the trend in market share, the ability to generate sales, the company size, its geographic, customer and product, its reputation: image, brand, etc. and its distribution and customer and supplier relationships.

Coca Cola has the largest market share in the soft drink industry (40% in the U.S.) operates in over 200 countries, has the number one ranked global brand (Coca Cola) with an estimated value of $78 billion (compared to intangibles valued at $24 billion on its balance sheet).

Cost position / operating efficiency: Cost position/operating efficiency consists of a company's ability of add value due to its supply chain / vendor management, assets and other resources. The simplest measure of a company's ability to add value is its return on its capital employed. If a company's return on capital is high, it can attract more capital if necessary. A company at least has to offer a higher return on capital than the return on government bonds. Investors would rather invest in risk free government bonds rather than a company if the company's returns were not greater than those of government bonds were. As a rough guide, most companies try to obtain a 10% return on capital employed. If they do not feel they can earn more than 10% they will return the money to shareholders in the form of dividends or share buybacks. For the past five years Coca Cola' return on capital employed has averaged about 20%.

Management

Management is evaluated by its by its absolute historical operating and financial performance, its historical performance relative to its peers, its controls/information systems, and succession planning and its special ownership characteristics. Coca Cola's past performance has equaled or bettered that of Pepsi.

Rating agencies evaluate a management's strategy by its realism, challenges and implementation. In general, industries and companies with strong business positons tend to attract conservative managements. Their performance is predictable. In contrast, industries and companies with vulnerable business positions tend to attract less conservative managements because their business is less predictable. However conservative or aggressive does not imply good or bad management. Businesses with high risk for example, can offer high returns to shareholders. In contrast, creditors make no more when a business does exceptionally well than when it performs evenly and steadily. Only equity shareholders benefit from high returns.

Coca Cola's business strategy is to use its assets including its brands, its financial strength, its unrivalled distribution strength, its global reach, and its strong commitment of management and employees, to become more dominant and to accelerate growth in a manner that creates value for its shareholders. This is a strategy it has been using for years and has been applying successfully.

Conclusion

For the Rating agencies, the degree of a firm's business risk sets the parameters of financial risk it can afford at any rating level and therefore they view industry analysis as critical. As a result, rating agencies divide responsibility for corporate ratings by industry, not by credit quality (investment grade versus non-investment grade), geographic area (Japan vs. U.S.) or type of loan (secured versus unsecured.) The exception was structured finance where the rating agencies divided the work for analysts by type of asset — Residential Mortgages, Credit Cards, Student Loans, and Auto Loans etc. not by industry - real estate, autos, etc.

Parent/Subsidiary Links

Rating agencies rate subsidiaries as well as parent companies. Their fundamental assumption is that the primary factor determining whether a parent will support its subsidiary, or a subsidiary will support a parent, is economic self-interest.

Strong Parent with Weak Subsidiary

The most common situation is a strong parent with a weak subsidiary. Indications of an implicit willingness to provide support to a subsidiary under a stress scenario include a strategic relationship, a significant ownership, management control, viability, historical support, operational integration and identification.

- *Strategic relationship: -* Rating agencies view the parent as likely to support a subsidiary if the subsidiary is a logical fit within parent's strategy and goals and if the parent's strategy has been in place for a reasonable time.

- *Ownership and management control:* Rating agencies view the parent as likely to support a subsidiary if there is a commitment and economic incentive to support the subsidiary and if the parent has the ability to influence and take the necessary action.

- *Significance:* Rating agencies view the parent as likely to support a subsidiary if the investment is large and the subsidiary is a significant part of the parent's overall current and historical business.

- *Viability:* Rating agencies view the parent as likely to support a subsidiary if the subsidiary has a substantial position within its markets, is sufficiently profitable, adequately capitalized and operates as a viable business without constant parent support.

- *History:* Rating agencies view the parent as likely to support a subsidiary if there is a history of the parent providing support to all of its subsidiaries.

- *Operational Integration:* Rating agencies view the parent as likely to support a subsidiary if the parent and subsidiary share common systems (e.g. manufacturing, distribution, and technology), management (board members, executives) and other non-financial resources.

- *Identification:* Rating agencies view the parent as likely to support a subsidiary if there is a commonality of corporate names since a common name is a strong intangible form of support and results in a recognition by investors and the public of the linkage between the parent and the subsidiary. A common name indicates a certain pride of ownership implicit in the parent/subsidiary relationship. While this point seems simplistic, studies of past subsidiary defaults shown a substantially greater frequency of default for non-parent named subsidiaries than for parent named subsidiaries.

Conclusion: If, after reviewing the above factors, rating agencies conclude there is strong support they may upgrade a subsidiary from BB to BBB with an A parent. On the other hand, if the parent has large weak subsidiaries rating agencies may downgrade the parent's own rating. For example, rating agencies may downgrade a AA parent with a large weak B subsidiary to a A+ and upgrade the weak subsidiary to BB.

Rating agencies give little weight to weak explicit support like comfort letters or maintenance agreements that call for minimum net worth, cash flow or performance.

Rating agencies base their ultimate assessment on the probability of default and the degree of support (none, partial, full). Rating agencies also consider the timeliness of the support, whether the support is in cash or liquid securities, whether support is retained as long as the debt is outstanding and if the subsidiary is sold whether or not equivalent support is substituted or the ex-parent support is maintained. With a guarantee, rating agencies substitute the parent's creditworthiness for that of the weaker subsidiary in countries where courts enforce guarantees. However, not all guarantees are equal! Legal enforcement varies from country to country.

Weak Parent with Strong Subsidiary

If there is a weak parent but a strong subsidiary, rating agencies apply a consolidated rating if the "single economic entity concept" applies. Bankruptcy filings by industrial parent companies, more often than not, include their subsidiaries. There can be a higher rating for a subsidiary if there is clear and compelling justification. The upgrade is usually limited to one rating category (BBB to A).

Subsidiaries may often be rated higher than the parent if the parent is a Single Purpose Corporation (SPC), there is regulatory separation, the parent is a pure holding company (a portfolio or businesses) or the parent is a non-captive finance company. When there is foreign ownership with different bankruptcy codes, the parent bankruptcy would not necessarily prompt the subsidiary's bankruptcy. However, rating agencies always evaluate the parent's credit quality.

When there is a weak parent with a/strong subsidiary, rating agencies' rating gap is usually less than one category (e.g., B- / BB-). This narrower rating gap is because of the danger that the parent could withdraw a subsidiary's resources. When there is a strong parent with a weak subsidiary, rating agencies may give a larger rating gap for foreign subsidiaries than for domestic subsidiaries because it is easier for parent to distance itself from a foreign subsidiary's problems

Chapter 3: Rating Agency Credit Analysis (Financial Risk)

The rating agencies corporate credit financial risk rating process is <u>*comparative.*</u>

- The <u>*quantitative approach*</u> uses financial statements as reported adjusting for accounting practices as well as cross-border differences.
- The <u>*qualitative approach*</u> adjusts for relative consistency and comparability.

The rating process uses historical financial reports — usually 5 years of audited statements. Exceptions occur when comparisons are less meaningful including corporate credits in countries where there is hyperinflation, where there is privatization or when the corporate credit is a new business.

For all credits, two to three years of projections that include a detailed statement of assumptions, sensitivities and scenarios are preferred. Obviously, large highly rated companies usually do not feel it necessary to provide projections and prefer to keep them confidential. For non-investment grade credits, detailed projections are required. In general, corporates need to be as forthcoming and open as possible. This is because once a company has mislead rating agencies they will find it difficult to regain their trust. Generally, it is in the corporate's and rating agencies self- interest to have accurate and stable ratings.

Financial ratios are not hurdles or prerequisites to a specific debt rating. Rating agencies evaluate ratios on an absolute basis, in comparison to peers, in comparison to other industries, based on their trend and based on the stage of economic and industry cycles.

Accounting rules do provide corporates with some latitude in the way they report their numbers for reporting purposes. Therefore, one of the challenges of the rating agencies is to make adjustments between peers if companies within an industry use different accounting methods. Examples include accounting for *inventories*: LIFO - last in-first out or FIFO - first in-first out, <u>*depreciation:*</u> - straight line or accelerated, and *research and development* — expensed or amortized over three years. For tax purposes, corporates use the most conservative method possible to reduce their taxable income. The difference between the reported income and taxable income is included as deferred taxes on the corporate's balance sheet.

Rating agencies adjust financial ratios to reflect *on-going operational profitability and cash flows.* Standard adjustments include adjustments for:

- Nonrecurring gains and losses
- Un-remitted equity earnings of a subsidiary
- Unusual cash flow items that affect funds flow ratios
- Operating leases
- "Excess" cash, and
- Captive Finance Companies

Areas of concern for rating agencies occur when there is:

- A lack of sufficient disclosure and transparency
- Overly aggressive accounting policies and earnings management practices
- Fraud and failure of internal control systems to detect and prevent irregularities
- A deterioration of audit practices and conflicts of interest
- Increasingly complex financial products, including "engineered" transactions involving form over substance, and/or
- Corporate governance scandals

Another challenge is evolving accounting standards that make analysis more complex including:

- Mark-to-market Accounting (SFAS 133 and 138)
- Reporting Special Purpose Entities (SFAS 94) and (FASB Interpretation No. 46)
- Securitized Assets Accounting (SFAS 140)
- Accounting for Intangibles and Goodwill (SFAS 141 and 142)
- Reiteration of rules for disclosing guarantees (FASB Interpretation No. 45)
- SEC rules
- Potential convergence of GAAP and IAS.

It is important to remember, rating agencies *rely on issuers and their auditors* for providing financial information. Rating agencies base their ratings on their analytical views, not just the reported figures and, in their view, accounting changes *should not* lead to rating changes unless they reveal new risks. Rating agencies scrutinize a corporation's method of reporting revenue, cost capitalization, and off-balance sheet items and adjust for "earnings management" practices.

Rating agency corporate financial risk analysis evaluates five areas:

- Financial Policy
- Profitability and profitability ratios
- Cash Flow Protection and cash flow ratios,
- Capital Structure and capital structure ratios, and
- Financial Flexibility/Liquidity

Adjusted financial ratios for profitability, cash flow and capital structure are important inputs to rating agency ratings. While relevant ratios vary somewhat from industry to industry, rating agencies rely heavily on seven key ratios that correlate most closely for ratings across industries. These seven key ratios consist of two profitability ratios, four cash flow ratios and one capital structure ratio. Estimates for these ratios over a 3-5 year period in the future for investment grade credits and 12-18 months for non-investment grade credits heavily influence's ratings. Listed below in bold are the seven key ratios in the sections on profitability, cash flow and capital structure. Other important ratios are listed in regular type.

Financial Policy

Financial policy consists of management's philosophies and policies and provides the context in which to view financial performance. For the rating agency, meetings with senior management are central to financial policy assessments. The primary concern is whether managements are creditor oriented or shareholder oriented.

Credit oriented managements are conservative. If they make an acquisition, they acquire it with stock. They tend to retain earnings, have low dividend payout ratios and do not repurchase their stock. Shareholder oriented managements are aggressive. If they make an acquisition, it is with debt. They have high dividend payout ratios and repurchase their stock.

Coca Cola has high dividend payout ratios and repurchases substantial amounts of its own stock. However, it also generates sufficient discretionary cash flow to cover these disbursements. Therefore, the rating agencies generally view Coca Cola's Financial Policy as strong or A.

Profitability

Profitability is a key factor in creditworthiness. Profitability generates internal equity capital, attracts external capital, represents a cushion to adverse business trends and attests to asset values.

The key profitability ratios (as adjusted) are return on capital (%), EBIT interest coverage (x) and Operating income / Sales (%).

Return on capital (%) is earnings before interest and taxes divided by average of beginning of year and end of year capital (debt +equity). High returns on capital indicate undervalued assets. Low returns on capital suggest overvalued assets.

EBIT / Interest Coverage (x) is earnings from Continuing Operations before Interest and Taxes / Interest Expense. It is widely used to analyze investment grade companies because it assumes these companies are strong enough to obtain financing for needed working capital or capital expenditures. It reflects the firm's long-term flexibility and ability to cover interest. It is not as useful in analyzing speculative-grade firms

Operating income/Sales (%) varies across industries and is therefore only helpful for evaluating companies within an industry or evaluating a company's individual performance over time.

Cash Flow

Cash flow is a key factor in determining creditworthiness - in meeting debt service and other obligations and contributing to liquidity. A high growth company can be profitable and still have weak cash flow. Therefore, rating agencies evaluate cash flow differently in low and high growth scenarios.

- (EBITDA -- earnings before interest and taxes plus depreciation and amortization
- FFO (Funds from Operations -- net income (after tax) plus depreciation, amortization, deferred income taxes, and other non-cash Items
- OCF (Operating Cash Flow - funds from operations minus (plus) increase (decrease) in *working capital* (excluding changes in cash, near-cash, and short term debt)
- FOCF (Free Operating Cash Flow - operating cash flow minus *capital expenditures*
- DCF (Discretionary Cash Flow - free operating cash flow minus *dividends*

XYZ Corporation Example of Cash Flow Measures

$ Millions	Year One	Year Two
Net Income from operations after tax	$14.3	$13.8
+ *Depreciation*	+$ 3.2	+$ 3.2
+ *Deferred Tax*	+$ 1.1	+$ 2.0
Funds from operations (FFO)	+$18.6	+$19.3
+ *Dec. (- increase) in non-cash current assets*	-$33.1	-$ .1
+ *Inc. (- decrease) in non-debt current liabilities*	+$15.1	-$ 7.6
Operating cash flow	+$ 0.6	+$12.7
-*Capital expenditures*	-$11.1	-$ 5.7
Free operating cash flow	-$10.5	+$7.0
-*Cash dividends*	-$ 4.5	-$ 5.1
Discretionary cash flow	-$15.0	+$ 1.9

The key cash flow ratios are EBITDA / Interest Coverage (x), FFO/Total Debt (%), Free Operating Cash Flow / TD (%) and Total Debt / EBITDA (x).

EBITDA /Interest Coverage (x) is a ratio that calculates operating cash flow coverage of interest payments to debtholders. Rating agencies emphasize this ratio in the evaluation of leveraged transactions. Adjustments to this ratio can include dividends for debt-like preferred stock. The ratio's shortcoming is that it does not account for capital expenditures and working capital requirements.

FFO / Total Debt (%) is a high-level ratio for cash flow leverage. The ratio's shortcoming is that it does not account for capital expenditures and working capital requirements.

FOCF/Total debt (%) is a ratio that calculates cash flow leverage in a way that includes working capital and capital expenditures. The ratio is applicable for high growth and capital-intensive companies. The ratio's shortcoming is that it does not include dividends.

Total Debt / EBITDA (x) is the most important ratio for evaluating speculative-grade companies. The ratio provides a cash flow measure of leverage. The ratio's advantages over traditional balance sheet measures of leverage is that there are fewer distortions associated with historical cost-based accounting. The ratio compares the balance sheet value of debt with the cash flow generation in current currency. The ratio is applicable even for companies with a negative net worth.

Supplemental cash flow ratios include Operating Cash Flow / Total Debt (%), Discretionary Cash Flow / Total Debt (%) and Funds from Operations / Capital Spending Requirements (x).

The relevance of different cash flow ratios varies along the rating spectrum.

Limitations of these ratios occur when rating agencies apply them to low growth companies or companies with a declining market share. In these cases there can appear to be strong cash flows because there are minimal fixed and working capital needs. There is the danger that the company might not be able to sustain this high level of protection. In contrast, for high growth companies there may be thin or negative cash flow because the investment is supporting growth. The key question is evaluating the prospects of enhanced cash flow protection once current investment begins yielding cash benefits.

Capital Structure

A company's capital structure is a summary of its total funding. The capital structure provides information on the sources of funding and the priority of claims. Rating agencies determine the value of a company by the long-term earnings power of its assets. Given the difficulty of measuring asset values in liquidation, rating agencies place a greater emphasis on evaluating a company's estimated future cash flow.

Capital structure measures and key ratios are total debt / total debt + equity, total debt + off-balance sheet liabilities/ total debt + off-balance sheet liabilities + equity and market value/book value.

The Total Debt / Total Debt + Equity (%) ratio provides an unambiguous starting point for determining the relative commitments among capital providers. The ratio's shortcomings are that the values represent historical accounting and are meaningless for negative book equity companies.

The Total Debt + Off Balance Sheet Liabilities/Total Debt + Off Balance Sheet Liabilities + Equity ratio adjusts for lease/purchase differences and more accurately reflects asset protection and financial leverage based on historical accounting.

The Market Value/Book Value (%) *ratio takes into account the market's assessment of future cash flows. The ratio's shortcoming is that values may be volatile as markets fluctuate.* Rating agencies do not include this ratio as a key ratio but it helpful as a quick check on how the equity market evaluates the future earning power of a company's assets.

Off-balance sheet liabilities that rating agencies often need to adjust for in calculating ratios include operating leases, guarantees, and other debt-like contingencies, receivables financing, captive finance company debt, non-recourse debt (e.g. joint ventures, affiliates) and take or pay obligations.

Operating Leases: There are two main analytical approaches to adjust for operating leases:

- the Net Present Value (NPV) method that rating agencies use if information is available, and
- the Factor Method, in absence of supplementary leasing information — for example -- eight times annual rents.

Accounts receivable sale/securitization: Standard adjustments for accounts receivable sale/securitization depend upon the form of off balance sheet financing. The normal practice is to add back the receivables sold with a similar amount of debt on the balance sheet. The sales discount (interest cost) is then classified as a part of a company's interest expense. The financial impact is neutral if the sale supplants other debt. However, rating agencies assume the financial risk increases if the company invests the funds in riskier assets.

Captive Finance Companies: A captive finance company is a finance subsidiary that generates >70% of its receivables by its parent's sales. Capital goods producers, auto manufacturers and retailers frequently use captive finance companies to increase sales. However, most companies do not consolidate their captive finance companies. If a company should capitalize its captive finance company (like Volkswagen, for example) the rating agencies remove it to make it more like other companies within the auto industry.

The analytical approach used by rating agencies to adjust for captive finance companies is to balance / re-balance the capital structure between the captive finance company and the parent until they are both approximately the same rating. The captive finance company's receivables can usually support a higher debt burden for a given rating level than a non-financial company. However, the captive finance company's rating can never be above the parent rating.

For the rating agencies, overall ratings correlate by Business Risk Profile relative to coverage benchmarks such as operating cash flow/total borrowed funds.

Operating Cash Flow/Total Borrowed Funds (%) And Business Position And Approximate Overall Rating

Coca Cola's operating cash flow/total borrowed funds is about 45% and with its strong business risk profile the ratio suggests an A+ to AA- overall rating.

Overall Rating	AAA	AA	A	BBB	BB
Excellent business risk profile	>60	45-60	30-45	15-30	>15
Strong business profile	-	>60	45-60	30-45	15-30
Satisfactory/fair business profile	-	-	>60	45-60	30-45
Weak business profile	-	-	-	>60	
Vulnerable business profile	-	-	-	-	>60

The table below summarizes the seven key financial ratios discussed above that have historically most closely correlated with credit ratings. Four of the ratios are cash flow ratios and one is a profitability ratio. Listed in bold are the ratios that are most closely correlate with Coca Cola's ratios.

Seven Key Industrial Financial Ratios for Long Term debt

Three year (2002 to 2004 medians	AAA	AA	A	BBB	BB	B	CCC
1. EBIT interest coverage (x)	23.8	19.5	8.0	4.7	2.5	1.2	0.4
2. EBITDA interest coverage (x)	25.5	24.6	10.2	6.5	3.5	1.9	0.9
3. FFO/total debt (%)	203.3	79.9	48.9	35.9	22.4	11.5	5.0
4. Free operating cash flow/total debt (%)	127.6	44.5	25.0	17.3	8.3	2.8	(2.1)
5, Total debt/EBITDA (x)	0.4	0.9	1.6	2.2	3.5	5.3	7.9
6, Return on capital (%)	27.6	27.0	17.5	13.4	11.3	8.7	3.2
7. Total debt/total debt + equity (%)	12.4	28.3	37.5	42.5	53.7	75.9	113.5

The Coca Cola key ratios do not include the EBIT interest coverage ratio and the total debt/total debt + equity (%) ratios included in the industrial financial ratios above that are helpful for many companies. It does not include the EBIT interest coverage ratio because Coca Cola has large amounts of cash overseas that earn interest at rates substantially higher than the interest it pays in the US. Therefore, on a net interest expense basis it has extremely high or in some years negative EBIT interest coverage ratio. It does not include the Total debt/total debt + equity (%) ratio because Coca Cola's has substantially reduced its equity by stock buy backs over the years. As a result, Coca Cola has a market value of common/book value ratio in excess of five times suggesting the book equity is grossly understated.

Cola Co. Key Financial Ratios for 2012 -2014

Adjusted Ratios	2012	2013	2014	Avg.	Rating	Outlook
1. CASHFLOW EBITDA interest coverage (x)	24.1	22.4	21.7	22.7	AA-	Stable
2. CASHFLOW FFO/total debt (%)	49.9	47.9	38.9	45.6	A-	Stable
3. CASHFLOW Free operating cash flow/total	36.6	35.7	30.7	34.3	A+	Stable
4. CASHFLOW Total debt/EBITDA (x)	1.7	1.7	2.1	1.8	A	Stable
5. PROFITABILITY Return on Capital (%)	21.8	20.1	16.4	19.4	A	Stable
6. MARKET VIEW Market value of common/book	5.0	5.2	6.1	5.4	?	Stable

The table above summarizes Coca Cola's Key Financial Ratios, their correlations with industrial financial ratios, and the outlook for these ratios over the next 3-5 years

Based on the above ratio's Coca Cola has an A cash flow financial rating and an A profitability rating. Its capital structure rating is also about an A rating although this is distorted by the fact it is indirectly responsible for the debt of its bottlers who have higher financial risk than Coca Cola.

Flexibility/Liquidity

Financial flexibility and liquidity are resources designed to protect the credit worthiness of company during sources of sudden adversity. Examples of sources of sudden adversity include:

- Real or alleged management impropriety
- Announced or suspected accounting abuses
- Dramatic business setbacks
- Adverse litigation
- Catastrophic derivatives / trading losses, and
- Sovereign interventions.

Examples of other potential demands on liquidity include:
- Term-related demands from long-term debt maturities and short-term debt usage
- Operations-related demands from contractually committed capital expenditures and working capital needs
- Pension and healthcare demands, and
- Off balance sheet obligations

Internal sources of liquidity to meet demands on liquidity include:
- Surplus cash / liquid Assets
- Capital asset sales
- Scaled back operations
- Reduced capital expenditures
- Reduced dividends
- Improvements in efficiency & margins, and
- Parental support

External sources of liquidity include:
- Trade credit
- Lines of credit
- Private placements
- Public bond market, and the
- Common stock market

Bank Lines are a critical source of liquidity and are based on:
- Unused committed facilities
- Bank relationships
- Syndicated bank groups
- Long term debt, and an
- Absence of covenants and debt "triggers"[1]

Other considerations that can constrain liquidity are:
- Small company size
- Legal problems
- Environmental problems
- Insurance requirements
- Debt maturities
- Pension obligations

Non-Investment Grade Credit

Rating agencies place a different emphasis on parts of their rating methodology when evaluating non-investment grade debt. For business risk, they place greater emphasis on financial plans, management and ownership. For financial risk, they place greater emphasis on discretionary cash flow and financial flexibility.

Non-investment grade debt has a higher volatility in credit quality than investment grade debt. Therefore, rating agencies change non-investment grade ratings more frequently. In addition, non-investment grade debt is more volatile in price, less liquid and requires closer portfolio monitoring. Investors in non-investment grade bonds should be limited to highly sophisticated investors.

Examples of companies with non-investment grade ratings include:

- Start-up companies with high financial risk and/or start up risk. Examples include high growth companies, telecommunications companies and tech companies.

- Companies in high-risk industries with high business risk. Examples include commodity companies and cyclical companies.

- Highly leveraged companies with very high financial risk. Examples include "LBO" (leveraged buyout) restructurings.

- Companies in emerging markets with high sovereign or country risk. Examples include Eastern European media companies with high regulatory risk.

Projected cash flows are key to evaluating non-investment grade corporate transactions. Key variables need to be stress tested and the opportunities for cost savings (margin improvement) evaluated. For start-ups, rating agencies evaluate the business plan, compare it with others in the industry/market, and evaluate management's previous operating experience.

The analysis emphasizes short-term financial risk. Rating agencies cannot assume refinancing will be available and therefore expect companies to have the internal ability to meet operational requirements including maintenance capital expenditures and working capital requirements as well as debt service (principal and interest) requirements.

There is a reliance on cash flow - a focus on EBITDA and discretionary cash flows (internal sources) to repay debt. Often the balance sheet may undervalue assets, and distort traditional capitalization measures. There are often complex capital structures that reflect the need for capital that exceeds "straight debt" availability. Therefore, there are often junior issues that provide a cushion for senior issues. However, the value of that cushion depends upon the enforcement of seniority rights under local bankruptcy laws

Rating agencies evaluate financial flexibility for non-investment grade credits based on the availability of bank lines, the access to capital markets and the capacity for asset disposals and sponsor funding.

Conclusion

Unfortunately, rating agencies never state precisely how they rate different aspects of a company's credit. Rather than saying a company's industry, competitive position or management is a AAA they say its industry, competitive positon or management are "Excellent".

Standard & Poor's "Corporate Rating Scale

S&P rates the carbonated soft drink industry Strong (AA) due to its stable performance, slow growth, high margins and brands. They rate Coca Cola's competitive position Strong (AA) as well because of its large market share, geographic distribution, and strong brands. Finally, they rate its management Strong (AA) because of its past stable performance and strong cash flows.

S&P rates Coca Cola's Financial Policy *Intermediate* or A-, its Profitability *Modest+* or A+, its Cash Flow *Modest* or A+, its Capitalization *Modest* or A and its Financial Flexibility *Modest* or A.

Combining its AA *"Strong"* business profile with it A+ *"Modest +"* financial profile S&P rates Coca Cola AA-.

Rating	Business Risk Profile	Financial Risk Profile
AAA	Excellent	Minimal
AA	Strong	Modest
A	Satisfactory	Intermediate
BBB	Fair	Significant
BB	Weak	Aggressive
B	Vulnerable	Highly Leveraged

Business/Financial Risk Weightings

Financial Risk / Business Risk Profile	Minimal	Modest	Intermediate	Aggressive	Highly Leveraged
Excellent business position	AAA	AA	A	BBB	BB
Strong business position	AA	A	A-	BBB-	BB-
Satisfactory business position	A	BBB+	BBB	BB+	B+
Weak business position	BBB	BBB-	BB+	BB-	B
Vulnerable business position	BB	B+	B+	B	B-

As you can see from the above table, the rating agencies will almost never rate a company with an excellent business position below a BB nor do a company with a vulnerable business position a rating higher than a BB.

"Issue" Ratings ("Notching")

Business entities can have multiple layers of obligations that rating agencies rank by priority claims on assets in bankruptcy.

Rating agencies base the <u>Issuer Rating</u> or Corporate Credit Rating ("CCR") on the default risk. The Issuer Rating is the baseline for notching <u>Issue Ratings</u>. Rating agencies base the Issue Rating on the default risk and the recovery prospects in default. Notching reflects the relative recovery potential. However, notching pertains only to differentiating recovery prospects. It is not a prediction of a "specific" recovery level.

Business entities can have multiple layers of obligations that rating agencies rank by priority claims on assets in bankruptcy.

Debt secured with higher-quality operating assets   **Most Senior**

Debt secured with lower-quality operating assets

Senior debt of the operating company

Senior liabilities at the operating company (pari-passu w/senior debt)

Subordinated debt

Junior subordinated debt

Senior debt of the holding company

Subordinated debt of the holding company   **Most Junior**

The more senior the debt, the greater the recovery prospects. Rating agencies typically notch long-term ratings down if the debt is:

- Secured, but secured by inferior collateral
- Unsecured, with secured debt ahead of it
- Contractually subordinated
- Structurally subordinated (e.g., debt at a holding company)

For notching, the disadvantage to specific issue must be <u>*material.*</u> Rating agencies do not notch down short-term ratings.

The maximum notching for debt issues is one notch for investment grade, e.g. A => A- and two notches for non-investment grade, e.g. BB => B+. There is No further notching among different classes of subordinated debt instruments. However, further notching down may occur for preferred stock and other deferred payment instruments. The reason notching for investment grade credits is limited to one notch is that the possibility for default for these credits is so low. On the other hand, the default rate for non-investment grade credits is much higher and therefore the notching can be up to two notches.

There are two types of subordination - contractual subordination and structural subordination. Contractual subordination is based on the loan contract - i.e. this loan is senior to other loans, or subordinated to other loans, is secured by XXXX, or is unsecured. Structural subordination means that the loan is at the holding company level, not the operating subsidiary level. (According to most countries bankruptcy laws, operating subsidiary obligations are senior to holding company obligations.)

Bankruptcy law permits structurally subordinated obligations to become more senior through upstream guarantees, downstream loans, operating assets at the parent, diversity and/or concentration of debt at a single subsidiary. The framework assumes a well-functioning national bankruptcy system.

Bank Loan Ratings and Evaluating Distressed Debt

The "business risk" and "financial risk" methodology, is best suited for evaluating investment grade credits (BBB- or better) where the probability of default is low. On the other hand, banks mostly lend to noninvestment grade credits (BB+ or lower) but make the expected loss manageable through higher interest rates, covenants, collateral and their ability to work with clients when a credit deteriorates. The bank analysis for these non-investment grade loans is different than the analysis for investment grade credits.

Each bank has its own internal rating system and method for evaluating their loan exposures. However, their methodology starts with default ratings that they then adjust into expected loss ratings after considering the degree to which structural elements mitigate risks.

The corporate credit rating or issuer rating is the starting point and the baseline for default risk. The debt cushion is the proportional amount of debt of inferior position to the loan or security rated, whether the debt is senior, subordinated, secured or unsecured. Past studies have shown a close correlation in ultimate recovery in the U.S. between senior secured debt and junior subordinated debt. According to S&P"s Loss Stats senior secured bank debt has had a recovery of 78% of par value compared to only 22% for junior subordinated notes.

Average Ultimate Recovery after Default*
% of Par Value at Emergence from Bankruptcy

	%	#
Senior Secured Bank Debt	78	795
Senior Secured Notes	65	224
Senior Unsecured Notes	42	472
Senior Subordinated Notes	31	369
Subordinated Notes	30	352
Junior Subordinated Notes	22	<u>44</u>
All Instruments (Weighted average)	**53**	**2,256**

*Database Source: Standard and Poor's Loss Stats

Collateral consists of discrete assets that are valued by past market transactions or by current appraisals. The evaluation process takes into account the stability of values at different stages of the economic cycle and adjusts for liquidity, volatility, the relationship of value of the collateral to the value of the business, adjusts for the value of special purpose assets and adjusts for anticipated stress in values at the time of default

The analysis estimates the value of the company in distress (post default). There are three different possible default scenarios:

- *A strong business* with high leverage suggesting a recapitalization that reduces debt,

- *A weak business* with low leverage suggesting a liquidation of assets with high recoveries and
- *A weak business* with high leverage suggesting a liquidation of assets with significant losses.

Asset Type	Examples	Key Characteristics
Financial Assets	Cash Marketable Securities Accounts Receivable	Low cost to realize Established market Value independent of business
Inventory	Select Raw Materials Finished Goods	Commodity v. Specialized Easily liquidated Technological risk
Personal Property	Transportation Equipment Containers	Diversified pool Technological risk Established market Non-specialized
Real property	Supermarket Convenience Stores Industrial Plants Office Buildings	Location diversity Environmental exposure Local Support/sponsor

For *strong businesses*, recapitalization efforts involve:

- estimating future cash flow
- capitalizing these cash flows via a cash flow multiple
- subtracting priority claims, and
- comparing the residual value with the bank loan,
- and then evaluating covenants and legal considerations.

Rating agencies estimate future cash flows on the average level of future cash flows that the business can generate over time using historic EBITDA as the base and adjusting for structural changes in the industry and/or restructuring of the company. The assumptions and adjustment for a likely default scenario assume the default scenario cash flow equals projected interest expense on a fully drawn loan facility and excludes one-time charges and extraordinary items.

The multiples employed for the estimated EBITDA cash flows are derived from cash flow multiples of the borrower's peer group. EBITDA Multiples of 5x to 7x are common. The low end of the multiple range more appropriately reflects the depressing effect that a filing or threat of bankruptcy typically has on the markets.

Projected EBITDA's are adjusted for product liabilities, environmental liabilities, other secured debt (Industrial Revenue Bonds, Mortgage debt etc.) trade creditors with priority first claim and assumes the bank facility is fully drawn at the time of default.

Covenants are "promises," the borrow makes. They mitigate the creditor's risk in term commitments for commercial and financial risks. They are a common "control mechanism" imbedded in bank credit agreements, high yield bonds and other fixed income instruments, guarantees and other contracts.

Covenants set the original expectations of borrower and lender. They define the financial profile, maintain the yield (risk and return) and preserve lender options including the ability to refinance, the access to collateral, the right to the sale of the company and the requirement to maintain the creditor's rights vs. other creditors.

There are two basic types of covenants, maintenance covenants and incurrence covenants.

- "Maintenance" covenants include the maintenance of a minimum profitability, minimum cash flow, minimum liquidity, maximum leverage etc.

- "Incurrence" covenants include violations that result through the incurrence of debt, payment of dividends ("distributions"), sale or transfer of assets, extension of guarantees, granting of "negative pledges" or change of control.

The covenant violation by a borrower is a "default" if the lender refuses to waive it. "Acceleration" is a remedy available to lenders of term commitments and permits them to suspend any unused loan commitment, accelerate scheduled maturities, and make term loans immediately payable.

The public bank loan market is covenant intensive and renegotiation is a "product feature". For the investment-grade bond market, covenants, if any, are incurrence covenants such as a material adverse change clause. In contrast, the non- investment-grade bond market is covenant intensive and bank loan designs do not feature renegotiation as a "product feature".

Bank loan agreements are contracts with collateral and other security requiring a perfection of security interests and an awareness of the practical issues involved in realizing value. They also have potential problems with inter-creditor issues, bank and client relationships, and lender liability and other matters.

Sovereign Risk & Country Risk

As mentioned in the beginning to Chapter 2, rating agencies use four stages to evaluate corporate credit ratings. The first stage is country risk, the second is business risk, the third is financial Risk and the fourth is issue risk.

Country risk is not relevant for the Coca Cola Case because the ratings for the United States is AA+ or AAA. For other countries, however the country risk rating effectively limits how high rating agencies will rate a corporate. For example, an emerging market country with a country risk rating of BB, in almost all cases, will limit the foreign currency ratings for its most creditworthy corporates to BB. For that reason, it is worthwhile to have an understanding of how rating agencies derive their country risk ratings.

Public Rating Agencies rate over 100 sovereigns. These ratings include global local currency and foreign currency sovereign ratings.

- The local currency sovereign rating rates the capacity and willingness of a country to meet its financial obligations denominated in its legal tender. The rating is determined by evaluating the country's fiscal performance, monetary performance, economic environment and political environment.

- The foreign currency sovereign rating rates the capacity and willingness of a country to meet its financial obligations in other than the country's legal tender. The rating is determined by evaluating all the above local currency ratings factors, plus external factors that may constrain foreign exchange access. Foreign currency denominated debt, therefore, generally has a higher default probability than local currency denominated debt.

There have been a number of large foreign currency defaults in the past 18 years.

Largest Sovereign Defaults since 1998

Country	Date	$Billion
• Greece	March 2012	$261
• Argentina	November 2001	$ 82
• Russia	August 1998	$ 73
• Puerto Rico	2015-2016	$ 70
• Greece	December 2012	$ 42
• Ukraine	October 2015	$ 18
• Jamaica	February 2013	$ 9
• Ecuador	August 1999	$ 7
• Uruguay	May 2003	$ 6

As of the end of 2015, rating agencies rate approximately 60% of emerging markets countries foreign currency rating speculative grade (BB+ or lower).

The rating agencies and banks express local and foreign currency debt ratings on a single scale for comparability to enable debt ratings to be of equivalent credit quality worldwide. Therefore, these rating agencies and bank ratings contrast with national scale ratings that local rating agencies apply solely within selected national markets.

Local currency company ratings evaluate the capacity and willingness of a corporate to generate sufficient local currency to meet all obligations subject to all sovereign risks, except transfer risk. *Sovereign risks* that *affect local currency ratings* include changing industrial, regulatory, fiscal and monetary policies. The impact of these policies can result in devaluations, price controls, a deteriorating regulatory environment, the temporary closing of the bank system, inflation / hyper-inflation, economic contraction, an acute credit shortage, political turmoil and higher taxation.

Foreign currency company ratings evaluate the capacity & willingness of a company to meet all its obligations including transfer risk. Foreign currency company ratings are therefore subject to all indirect and direct sovereign risks and transfer risks. *Transfer risks* that *affect foreign currency ratings* include exchange controls, frozen bank deposits, required repatriation of all funds held abroad, refusal to clear a transfer of funds, government-mandated moratorium /restructuring of principal and interest payments and different exchange rates for different types of transactions.

The assessment of an issuer's business environment includes an evaluation of the nature of the economic, operational, and competitive environment including an evaluation of whether the market is global, regional or mixed. Rating agencies evaluate whether the market is regional like retailing or global like energy and automobiles, export oriented like copper or local like telecommunications and whether local labor costs impair the company's international competitive position.

The evaluation process includes an assessment of an issuer's financial environment including its accounting system, adjustments to enable international comparisons, and ability to provide a US GAAP translation.

Because of accounting difficulties, non-US corporate ratings rely more on cash coverage of fixed financial charges and debt and less on abstract measures such as equity and reported earnings. Non-US corporations are not directly comparable with median published statistics. In addition, greater local ownership blocks provide positive and negative implications for any rating.

Economic/country risk encompasses the size, structure, growth and volatility of the economy, inflation/devaluation, labor costs, sensitivity to foreign investment, political stability, infrastructure, corruption and access to local capital.

We tend to think of the United States as a country that would never interfere with a bank's or corporate's ability to meet its foreign currency obligations. However, that is exactly what happened in 1974 when the US Government ordered all US banks to freeze any Iranian dollar deposits.

Rarely are bank foreign currency or local currency ratings greater than sovereign ratings because sovereigns regulate banks, have close economic ties with them and have the ability to impose bank defaults.

Rating agencies cap the majority of non-bank corporate ratings by the sovereign foreign currency and local currency ratings. However, in a few instances the corporates can mitigate the cap through parent company external guarantees, "safe haven" domiciles or geographic diversity of their subsidiaries. Historically, rating agency ratings of sovereigns have been equally as accurate as their ratings of corporates.

Sovereign and corporate default rates over one, three- and five-year intervals (% of rated issuers)

Rating	One-year		Three-year		Five-year	
	Sovereign	Corporate	Sovereign	Corporate	Sovereign	Corporate
AAA	0	0	0	0	0	0.1
AA	0	0	0	0.1	0	0.3
A	0	0	0	0.2	0	0.6
BBB	0	0.3	2.1	1.1	5.6	2.8
BB	1.1	1.1	5.6	6.0	8.8	10.7
B	3.0	5.4	8.8	17.1	17.6	24.2
CCC/CC	40.0	27.0	58.9	40.9	58.9	47.6

Standard & Poor's Sovereign Credit Ratings: A Primer, dated October 19, 2006, page 8.

Generally, there is a close correlation between a sovereign's per capita income and total GDP and its credit rating. Total GDP is an indication of political sophistication and the extent to which its domestic population can unite as a nation. Per Capita Income is an indication of the sophistication of a country's work force relative to other countries.

Sovereign Median per Capita Income by Rating Category* USD – 2006

AAA	39,000
AA	34,000
A	13,000
BBB	7,000
BB	3,000
B	1,000

* Standard & Poor's Sovereign Credit Ratings: A Primer, dated October 19, 2006, page 8.

Other indicators are the current account balance and net external debt as a % of exports. The current account balance is an indication of a country's sources of foreign currency relative to its needs for foreign currency. Net external debt as a % of exports is an indication of a country's historical ability to finance it needs for imports.

Current Account Balance as a % of Current Account Receipts* 2006

AAA	+7%
AA	+5%
A	+4%
BBB	-3%
BB	-6%
B	-13%

* Standard & Poor's Sovereign Credit Ratings: A Primer, dated October 19, 2006, page 14.

Net External Debt as a % of Exports (Current Account Receipts)* 2006

A	-20%
BBB	+30%
BB	+33%
B	+62%

*Standard & Poor's Sovereign credit Ratings: A Primer, date October 19, 2006, page 15

Long-term debt rating models give the highest weightings to total GDP and per capita GDP.

Long-Term Debt Rating Model as a Means of Assigning Country Risk Ratings

Key Factors	% Weighting
Total GNP	40%
Per Capita GNP	40%
Current account balance	10%
Net External Debt as a % of Exports	10%
TOTAL	100%

Short-term debt rating models give the heaviest weighting to net external debt as a % of exports.

Short-Term Debt Rating Model as a Means of Assigning Country Risk Ratings.

Key Indicator	% Weighting
Total GNP	20%
Per Capita GNP	20%
Current account balance	10%
Net External Debt as a % of Exports	50%
TOTAL	100%

Chapter 4:
Regulatory Credit Analysis

Regulators are concerned with three types of risks - credit risks, market risks and systemic risks. **Credit risks and credit cycles** are cyclical - recessions and booms and vary at different stages of an economic cycle. **Market risks and market cycles** accentuate credit cycles and result in increased volatility of prices for equities, commodities, homes etc. Studies of credit default swaps have shown that in recessions, market cycles, resulting from the uncertainty of the severity of economic cycles, are about three times as volatile as credit cycles. **Systemic risks and systemic cycles** accentuate market cycles, result in a lack of confidence in the banking system, and are about three times as volatile as market cycles or nine times as volatile as normal credit cycles.

Systemic cycles are extremely disruptive to economic growth and are the primary concerns of regulators. In systemic cycles, or "panics", regulators and central banks have to step forward and use taxpayer money to prop up the soundness of a country's financial system. In 2008-2009, the government and the regulators had to ask congress for $750 billion for a "Troubled Asset Relief Program" to bail out the U.S. banks. Foreign central banks faced similar crisis in their own countries and took similar actions.

As discussed earlier, systemic cycles are what global regulators are now determined to avoid in the future. They are central to the laws of Dodd- Frank and the current Basel III regulations. These laws and regulations are attempts to avoid the appearance in future recessions that the government will protect bankers but not individuals.

Technological progress, globalization, and a changed regulatory environment all contributed to the excessive optimism and debt of 2008-2009. **Technological progress** included technology and financial innovation including the Internet, the Web and a networked marketplace. **Globalization** included cross border mergers and acquisitions, communication and information technology that eroded trade barriers and led to a worldwide integration of banking and trading markets. The **Changed Regulatory Environment** included the break-down in fixed exchange rates, the deregulation of U.S. interest rates, the vanishing barriers between banking, investment banking, securities and insurance; broad and diverse financial products and an attempt to focus on risk management to compensate for these risks. These environmental changes led to an explosion in corporate bond and securitization activity between 1980 and 2000.

- Commercial paper increased from $0.1 trillion to $1.3 trillion an increase of 10X;
- Securitization increased from $0,006 trillion to $6.4 trillion an increase of 1000X;
- Corporate bonds increased from $1.5 trillion to $48.0 trillion and increase of 30X; and
- Traditional bank lending increased from $0.5 trillion to $5.6 trillion an increase of 10X.

These changes led to greater competition, downward pressure on loan margins, greater market volatility and increased stress on the risk management capabilities of financial institutions.

There were some warning signs that the global economy was becoming increasingly vulnerable to a systemic crisis.

Derivative Risk and Procter & Gamble: Derivatives were not the "cause" of the Procter & Gamble loss. Proctor and Gamble "gambled" by making a bet on interest rates, and it bet wrong. The Proctor and Gamble incident illustrated the interrelationships of risks: legal, operational, reputational. As a result, banking regulators increased their attention to the risk management challenges of derivatives to the banking industry.

Operational Risk - Barings Bank: Barings Bank was a classic case of inadequate operational controls. Barings Bank lack of operational controls enabled a single trader to create large market risk exposures. Regulators ultimately liquidated Barings Bank. As a result, banking regulators stepped up their attention to the risk management challenges of operational risk.

Liquidity Risk - Long-Term Capital Management: Long-Term Capital Management created enormous market and credit risk exposure to credit spreads between government bonds and corporate bonds in various countries. Because Russia devalued the ruble and declared a debt moratorium credit spreads widened, volatility increased, and liquidity evaporated. Long-Term Capital Management illustrated model risk, the need for stress testing and the resulting challenges of liquidity risk.

The Regulators Integrated View of Risk Management

From a regulatory perspective, risk management is a dynamic process that requires an integrated approach that identifies, measures, controls and monitors risk.

Identify Risk: Management must recognize and understand existing risks or risks that may arise from existing and new business initiatives, including risks that originate in non-bank subsidiaries. Management should follow identifying existing and potential exposure by identifying desired levels of risk exposure or risk tolerance. This process should be a continuing process, and should occur at both the transaction and portfolio level.

Measure Risk: Once management has identified the risks, a model can help quantify the risks. Quantifying risk means putting a value or price on risk, to help decide whether a risk is worth taking. Accurate and timely measurement of risk is essential to effective risk management systems. Without a risk measurement system, management has limited ability to control or monitor risk levels. The more complex the risk, the more sophisticated should be the tools that measure it. Management should periodically test measurement tools to ensure their validity. During a transition process resulting from bank mergers and consolidations, the effectiveness of risk measurement tools is often impaired because of the technological incompatibility of the merging systems or other problems of integration. Management must make a strong effort to ensure that it measures all risks appropriately across the consolidated entity. Larger, more complex companies must assess the impact of increased transaction volume across all risk categories.

Control Risk: Risk limits should be established and communicated through policies, standards, and procedures that define responsibility and authority. Control limits should be flexible to changes in conditions or risk tolerances. Managements should have a process to authorize exceptions or changes to risk limits when warranted. In banks merging or consolidating, management should tightly control the transition through clear business plans, lines of authority, and accountability. Large, diversified companies should have strong risk controls covering all geographies, products, and legal entities.

Monitor Risk: Managements should monitor risk levels to ensure timely review of risk positions and exceptions. Managements should distribute frequent, timely, accurate, and informative monitoring reports to appropriate individuals to ensure action, when needed. For large, complex companies, monitoring is essential to ensure that management implements its decisions for all geographies, products, and legal entities.

Risk Management Systems

Risk management systems include responsibility and authority, risk limits and controls, internal control procedures, reporting and monitoring and measurement systems that manage risks including credit, market and operational risks.

Types of Credit Risk

Credit Risk is the possibility of loss arising from obligor default or other adverse credit event. There are four types of credit risk - primary, pre-settlement, settlement and inventory.

Primary credit risk consists of <u>cash lending risk</u> where the principle is at risk and includes term and short term lending, illiquid debt securities, certificates of deposit, banker acceptances and committed/syndicated loans.

Pre-settlement risk consists of <u>potential future risk</u> where, in the event of default, banks need to replace trades and includes foreign exchange trades, options bought, swaps, bond trading up to settlement, forward rate agreements and collateralized lending.

Settlement risk consists of the <u>short-term risk</u> of not receiving the expected cash due to a default during the settlement process from foreign exchange trades, foreign exchange options and currency swaps.

Inventory risk consists of the <u>hold-to-maturity risk</u> of holding a bond while the issuer defaults and includes bond purchases and sales including sovereign debt.

Types of Market Risk

Market Risk is the possibility of loss arising from changes in prices/rates on bonds, stocks, currencies, commodities, etc. Market risk comes from the decrease in market value of securities held in the trading book and the banking book or from asset/liability gaps in the loan book. Market volatility determines the severity of market risk.

Types of Operational Risk

Operational Risk is the possibility of loss arising from failures in people, systems, processes and adverse external events.

Operational risk comes from transaction errors, criminal activity (theft, fraud), inadequate controls, catastrophic natural events, technological/system failure, regulatory/fiduciary violations and interconnections among major risk categories e.g. severe market risks stressing back office operations and increasing operational risks.

Management Challenges

Management challenges resulting from these risks include attempts to develop integrated risk management, the integration of risk and capital management, a board and senior management that determines risk- related capital objectives, and a senior management governance of conformity to risk and capital objectives.

The resulting trends in management from these challenges have been attempts to develop comprehensive, systematic, quantitative, analytical techniques for risk management of each risk class. These attributes have included volatility based techniques that enable unexpected loss determination for Value-at-Risk (VaR) and portfolio based risk management for each risk class and the ability to integrate the application of analytical techniques across risk classes.

The most successful and widely used technique to integrate risks across risk classes is the concept of Value-at-Risk (VaR). Value-at-Risk estimates the maximum loss that can be expected to occur no more than (1 - C) % of the time, where C = % confidence level. For example, a confidence level of 99% or one out of 100 days. VaR uses expected losses for exposures based on internal rating systems and the estimated historical % likelihood of default and/or loss for different rating categories. It attempts to estimate risks not only within a class of risk, but across classes of risk by adjusting for correlations between losses in different classes of risk. In other words, it adjusts for the probability that not every class of risk (i.e. credit, market, operational etc.) can deteriorate equally at the same time.

Internal Rating Systems:

The objective of internal rating systems is to determine <u>expected loss</u> for a specific facility. The expected loss (EL) is equal to the exposure at default (EAD) times the loss given default (LGD) times the probability of default (PD) i.e. EL=EAD X LGD X PD

Therefore, an internal rating system (IRS) should provide the obligor rating - the likelihood of default and the facility rating – the likelihood of loss given default.

- The <u>Obligor Rating</u> is an assessment of the likelihood that a particular issuer will be unable to meet its financial obligations when due.
- The <u>Facility Rating</u> includes, as well, an assessment of the likely loss on a particular facility in the event of a default by the issuer.

Internal rating systems are unique for each bank based on their individual historical experience. However, regulators expect a bank's internal ratings to correlate with the default and migration experience of Rating Agency ratings. The default internal ratings process of banks is similar to the default rating process of rating agencies.

Bank issuer - obligor ratings, like public rating agency ratings are based on a financial risk assessment derived from a company's financial statements, cash flow, profitability, organization, management, competitive industry position and country risk. (See Chapters 2 & 3.)

The bank issue - facility ratings, however, place a greater emphasis on the loan structure, subordination, third party support, collateralization and term.

Bank Facility Ratings - A Typical Approach

1	Low	AAA/Aaa	.00	Investment Grade
2	Low	AA/Aa	.01	
3	Low	A+/A+	.02	
4	Medium	A/A,BBB/Baa	.05	
5	Medium	BB/Ba	.20	Less Than Investment Grade
6	Medium	B+/B+	.50	
7	High	B/B	1.00	
8	High	CCC/Caa	3.00	
9	High	CC/Ca	6.50	
10	High	C/C	12.50	
11	Default	D	50.00	Non-Performing

History of the Basel I and II Capital Accords

The Basel I and II Capital Accords attempted to guarantee the safety of all banks by ensuring that they had a minimum amount of capital.

The Minimum Regulatory Capital Requirements started with a Standardized Approach for different types of credit exposures - loans, government securities, etc.

The 1988 Basel II Accord enhanced the capital requirements by imposing capital requirements not just by type of credit exposure but by the credit quality of the credit exposure. This approach — the Internal Ratings-Based (IRB) Approach had two frameworks — the **Foundation Framework** and the **Advanced Framework.** The Regulators determined which banks were eligible to apply for the IRB approach. In order to be eligible for the Internal Ratings-Based Approach a bank had to have:

- a risk rating system that could differentiate obligors and facilities into grades of similar credit risk,
- a distribution of exposures across all grades with no significant concentrations in any one grade,
- risk ratings that were used in the decision to make credit commitments,
- independent internal periodic review of risk ratings,
- board and senior management oversight of IRB framework, and
- a minimum of one-year default probability for each risk-rating grade.

Regulators will not accept banks for the IRB process until they have a historical database of all key data that demonstrates the accuracy of their ratings.

In 2008-2009, it became apparent that there were problems with the Internal Rated Based Approach to capital requirements. Basel II had assumed that:

IRB ratings for Risk Weighted Assets were accurate. In fact, this turned out to be wrong. In some cases, internally AAA rated credits that required almost no capital defaulted or increased in risk dramatically. The Basel III solution to the problem of over-inflated ratings is to require higher quality capital and more capital for highly rated credits.

Public debt markets reduce systemic risk. In 2008-2009, the collapse of public debt markets accentuated systemic risk because banks, as underwriters for much of the public debt had high inventories of these securities and had a contingent liability when they defaulted. The Basel III solution is increased requirements for bank liquidity.

The public debt markets reduced bank risk by reducing bank leverage. The banks used the public debt markets to sell loans and instead of reducing leverage with the proceeds, used the opportunity to make more loans. The Basel III solution is to increase capital requirements for systemically important financial institutions that issue public debt.

The size and diversification of Systemically Important Financial Institutions (SIFI) reduces their risk. The diversification of commercial banks into investment banking increased their risk by making them more vulnerable to market risks. The Basel III solution is to have holding companies for SIFIs to separate their commercial banking and investment banking activities in separate subsidiaries and raise much of their capital at the holding company parent as structurally subordinated capital. In addition, the Basel III solution requires SIFIs provide living wills that permit the holding company to fail without causing the systemically important operating commercial and investment banks to fail.

Banks under Basel II rules can survive independently of government support. A Congressional Committee concluded that, without the Troubled Asset Relief Program (TARP) 17 out of 18 of the largest US banks would have failed in 2008. As a result, Basel III doubled the capital requirements of the systemically important financial institutions.

Basel III for U.S. Banks

The U.S. banking industry is different from the banking industry in any other country. There are 7,000 banks - most countries have less than 10 banks. Only a dozen US banks participate significantly in derivatives and are too big to fail. In other countries, most banks participate in derivatives and are too big to fail. The US has well developed public debt markets, most other countries do not. Therefore, US regulators try to use public debt markets as a means of disciplining weaker banks. Formerly, regulators expected the public equity markets to provide the discipline to ensure that the banks would be prudent through their financing of their senior debt. With Basel III and the new holding company structure, the public debt markets are to provide the discipline indirectly through the bank's structurally subordinated debt at the holding company level. In the future, when the regulators take over a systemically important financial institution, the operating commercial and investment banks can continue to function without government financial support. The subordinated debt and equity holders at the holding company level will absorb all losses.

Basel III for all Banks

Basel III requires higher quality capital. The common equity portion for all bank's total capital requirement of 8% increased from 2 1/2% to 7%. Basel III also requires increased capital requirements for all banks through a 2 1/2% capital conservation buffer and a

2 1/2% countercyclical capital buffer bringing the total capital requirement for non-systemically important financial institutions up to 13%. However, for Systemically Important Financial Institutions (SIFIs) there is also a systemically important financial institutions buffer. These increases in Total Loss-Absorbing Capacity (TLAC) are to be phased in over the next several years. For non-emerging market economies it increases the TLAC in 3 to 6 years and for emerging market economies it increases the TLAC in 9 to 12 years.

Capital Conservation Buffer: The Capital Conservation Buffer, consisting exclusively of common equity, absorbs losses during periods of financial and economic stress. Banks that do not maintain the capital conservation buffer will face restriction on payouts of dividends, share buybacks and bonuses.

Countercyclical Capital Buffer: Each regulator according to national circumstances will implement the countercyclical capital buffer within a range of 0% - 2.5% of common equity or other fully loss absorbing capital. Regulators will view the countercyclical capital buffer when it is in effect as an extension of the capital conservation buffer.

SIFI Buffer: Basel III clearly recognizes that liquidation is not an option for large money center banks and much higher total capital ratios are required to permit SIFIs to survive as an on-going entity in a systemic crisis. For these SIFIs regulators add additional capital requirements depending upon the importance of the individual institutions to the overall economy.

In summary, Basel III increased capital ratios through the Conservation Buffer, the Countercyclical buffer, the SIFI Buffer and reduced eligible capital (required more common equity), increased the risk weighting of assets (for securitization products, etc.) and segregated the risk and capital management processes to ensure an adequate assessment of a firm's capital adequacy.

Basel III also initiated new capital requirements for counterparty credit risk management: These capital requirements include new Credit Value Adjustments and higher capital requirements for securitization products. For example, banks must clear derivatives and repos through a Counterparty Clearing Program (CCP) or face substantially higher capital requirements for each trade not cleared. In addition, regulators no longer view counterparty clearing houses as risk-free and require a 2% capital weight. In addition, clearing members must capitalize their share of a counterparty clearing houses default funds and use a higher correlation factor to internal ratings based approaches to risk weights. For secured lending there are also changes concerning collateral eligibilities and haircut rules.

Acceptable TLAC debt is debt that is subordinated to depositors and derivative liabilities. In the U. S. and UK, laws **structurally subordinate** this debt through holding companies, in some countries laws **contractually subordinate** this debt through debt contracts while in Germany and Europe laws directly **statutorily subordinate** this debt.

Basel III also requires new liquidity requirements for all banks including a liquidity coverage ratio and a new stable funding ratio.

Liquidity Risk: Liquidity risk is the most complicated challenge for regulators. The fundamental principle of bank earnings is borrowing short and lending long. In the US, with large public markets and the ability to sell bank equity short, runs on banks are inevitable. The discount window is essential and the Federal Reserve will always be required for liquidity. Nonetheless, the Basel III liquidity ratios are a good exercise, to keep banks aware of liquidity risks. Basel III attempts to address the issue of liquidity and funding by requiring minimum standards for <u>short-term liquidity funding</u> - the Liquidity Coverage Ratio (the LCR) and <u>long-term liquidity funding</u> - the Net Stable Funding Ratio (the NFSR").

Liquidity Coverage Ratio (LCR): The LCR is a short-term liquidity measure that identifies a firm's unencumbered, high-quality liquid assets (HQLA) that a bank can convert into cash to meet net cash outflows during a 30- day severe stress scenario.

Net Stable Funding Ratio (NSFR): The NSFR measures the amount of longer- term, stable sources of funding available to support the portion of all assets (on and off- balance sheet) that a bank cannot monetize over a one-year period of extended stress. While the LCR is to ensure that sufficient high quality liquid resources are available for a one month survival in case of stress scenario the Net NSFR promotes resiliency over longer-term time horizons by creating additional incentives for banks to fund their activity with more stable sources of funding on an ongoing structural basis. There are also additional liquidity monitoring metrics focused on maturity mismatch, concentration of funding and availability of unencumbered assets.

There are many challenges for banks from the Liquidity Risk Requirements. Banks will have to produce regulatory liquidity risk reports that will have to be produced a least monthly with the ability, when required by regulators, to deliver reports weekly or even daily. This requires banks to put in place robust automated reporting systems. The LCR and NSFR liquid asset eligibility and haircut rules rely on external ratings, Basel Classification of counterparties and standardized credit risk weights. The LCR and NSFR enumerate run-off rates and depend on information usually only available in risk specific systems and not treasury systems.

The increase in quantity and quality of capital, liquidity and leverage ratios, and capital preservation impacts all banks. Liquidity requirements especially affect sophisticated investment banks by the amended treatment of counterparty credit risk, the more robust market risk framework and to some extent, the amended treatment of securitizations. G-SIFIs will have to cope with additional loss-absorbing capital requirements and are subject to additional supervision.

Other Requirements: Finally, Basel III requires new structural requirements including living wills and separate investment banking subsidiaries. New capital, leverage and liquidity regulations are now in line with the Basel Committee rules, and are part of the Dodd Frank Act Amendment. All US banks are required to meet Basel III.

Financial Stability Board Standards

The Financial Stability Board (FSB) announced the final Standards on November 9, 2015. The FSB based its Standards on the results of four studies: a **Historical Loss Study** of SIFI's, an **Individual Bank Study** of each individual bank's costs of implementing the TLAC, an **Economic Impact Study** on the economic effects of implementing the TLAC, and a **Market Impact Study** on investor behavior and market capacity to implement the TLAC.

The FSB designed these studies to determine the amount of capital that would have been required, on average, to avoid taxpayer bailouts during the financial crises over the past 20 years and to determine the cost of implementing that increase in capital to the individual banks, to the economy and to the public debt markets.

The **Historical Loss Study** of failed SIFI's covered 13 banks, including Fortis, Merrill Lynch, Wachovia, Citi, Commerzbank, RBS, ING, UBS, B of A and three Japanese Banks. Eleven of the 13 banks were using Basel I Risk Weighted Assets at the time of government assistance. The Historical Loss Study concluded that while losses and recapitalization varied significantly, most losses and recapitalizations together were in the 4-6% range in terms of total assets (versus the TLAC Leverage Ratio of 6% and 6.75%) and in the 5-15% range in terms of Risk Weighted Assets (versus the TLAC 16% and 18%).

The **Individual Bank Study** focused on the costs of implementing the TLAC and found that the median increase in individual SIFI's borrowing rate to recoup the costs of the TLAC would be 5 bps for the 16% RWA and 6% Leverage Ratio and 8 bps for 18% RWA and 6.75% Leverage Ratio. These median rates would translates into an increase in lending rates for the average borrower of about 2 bps for the lower requirements and 3 bps for the higher requirements.

The **Economic Impact Study** focused on the costs of implementing the TLAC to the economy and found that the loss in annual GDP would be less than **2 bps** for the 16% RWA and 6% Leverage Ratio and **3 bps** for the 18% RWA and 6.75% Leverage Ratio requirements. On the other hand, the study estimated that the macroeconomic benefits to the TLAC were **48 bps** of annual GDP. The economic benefits were not only from the reduction in taxpayers losses but also from losses from unemployment etc.

The **Market Impact Study** on implementing the TLAC found that the aggregate TLAC shortfall represents only 1% to **2%** of the total €80 trillion global debt securities market and 17% to 31% of the €4.5 trillion SIFI issued unsecured debt market. Market participants estimated that the new issuance under the TLAC would cause bond spreads for SIFI's to rise 30 bps from the prevailing levels (versus 8 bps for the Federal Reserve Study).

Conclusion

The Glass Steagall Act required investment banks be separate from commercial banks. In the 1990's, large U.S. banks became more like non-U.S. banks - i.e. U.S. banks became universal banks with investment banking trading activities. In 2010, the Dodd-Frank law included the "swaps push-out" Volker Rule that prohibited proprietary trading in commercial banks. This law calls for the separation of commercial banks, with access to the discount window, from investment banks with no access to the discount window. There is public controversy over trading activities as speculative activities.

Rating Agencies evaluate the likelihood of default - *the ability to pay interest and principle to bondholders when due*. Ratings range from AAA to CCC. In the past, Regulators evaluated likelihood of loss to depositors and taxpayers (and other banks) through *the liquidation or sale of assets*. Small banks usually did not have public debt and so had a less diversified capital base and were therefore easier to liquidate. Large banks, however, had public equity, debt, preferred stock and enormous interbank obligations that were more difficult to liquidate. The crisis of 2008 demonstrated that large money center banks were too big to fail i.e. their failure would cause a systemic crisis. Therefore, regulators and legislators have tried to make the bank capital large enough to cover events like the Financial Crisis of 2008-2009 without losses for taxpayers. Like the rating agencies, the regulators now evaluate SIFI's on their ability to survive after a crisis, not just their ability to avoid a loss to taxpayers in liquidation after a crisis.

Chapter 5:
Bank Credit Analysis

The objective of this chapter on Bank Credit Analysis is to provide a methodology for evaluating:

- a country's economic and industry risk,
- how that risk assessment sets the parameters for all bank ratings within that country, and
- how to evaluate an individual bank's business risk and credit risk within those parameters.

The Chapter then applies that rating methodology to JP Morgan Chase.

Key Characteristics: The key characteristics of banks are that they are:

- Illiquid because they rely on short-term deposits and make longer term loans;
- Provide imperfect knowledge regarding borrowers and insufficient creditor information;
- Rely on system support and depositor protection from the government;
- Are highly leveraged making asset values critical rather than cash flows; and
- Under accrual accounting, have considerable latitude in recognizing losses.

Causes of Fragility: The primary causes of fragility in banking systems include change, poor institutional management, the danger of relying on implicit government support, deficient regulation, supervision, and enforcement and macroeconomic imbalances and volatility i.e. economic cycles.

INDIVIDUAL BANK RATING METHODOLOGY

Rating agencies evaluate a bank's business and financial risk in assessing its overall rating.

Business Risk

Rating agencies evaluate the following areas in assessing an individual bank's business risk:

Collective Bank Industry Business Risk Factors

Economic Risk Rating   _____
Industry Risk Rating   _____
Individual Bank Business Risk Factors

Market Position Rating   _____
Diversification Rating   _____
Management/Strategy Rating   _____
Overall Business Risk Rating _____

Collective Bank Business Risk Factors

Standard and Poor's' criteria use a "Banking Industry Country Risk Assessment" (BICRA) and the resulting economic and industry risk scores to determine a bank's anchor, the starting point for an issuer credit rating.

Economic Business Risks: The key risk for evaluating a country's banking system is the country's economic risks including:

- The size and nature of country's economy and its vulnerabilities
- Its growth prospects
- Its sensitivity to foreign investment
- Its openness to the global economy
- Its vulnerability to economic cycles and structural problems such as inflation and deflation

Highly rated countries include countries with strong growth prospects, non-cyclical industries and stable currencies. Industries increasing a country's cyclicality include industries with low sales to assets such as commercial real estate, residential real estate, banks, agriculture and commodities.

Sales/Revenues to Assets of U.S Entities

Wholesalers	300%
Industrials	180%
Heavy Industry	100%
Homes	33%
Utilities	30%
Real Estate	10%
Banks	?%
Investment Banks	?%
Agriculture/Commodities	?%

Put another way, expenditures with long shelf lives are more cyclical than expenditures with short shelf lives.

Expenditure	Shelf Life
Food	.1
Electronics	2.0
Machinery	3.0
Autos	5.0
Airplanes	20.0
Homes	50.0
Land/Farms	Infinite

Recessions/depression impose enormous strains on economies, especially in highly cyclical industries, as illustrated below for the 2008-2009 recession.

2008-2009 Key U. S. Economic Indicators

Indicator	12/31/07 US$	12/5/08 % Change	Change $ Trillions
GDP	13.5	-1%	-.1
Stocks	20.0	-40%	-8
Real Estate	30.0	-20%	-6
TARP Program	.8	+6%	+1
Congress Stimulus	1.0	+7%	+1

Important factors in evaluating a countries economic risk include evaluating the:

- Constraints on government's ability to pursue appropriate counter cyclical policies
- Country's political stability
- Dynamics of savings and investment
- Level and growth of domestic credit
- Structure and strength of corporate clients
- Financial strength of individual clients

Indicators of financial system stress within a country include rapid private and public credit growth, excessive corporate and household indebtedness, asset price inflation and external funding of financial institutions.

For example, Standard and Poor's rates the US economic risk rating for banks BBB+. It views the US as a diversified, high-income economy, with an adaptable and resilient economic structure. It believes the US continues in an expansionary phase, and that households appear to have moved beyond their multiyear deleveraging and are slightly more receptive to taking on debt, albeit more cautiously than in prior cycles. S&P view of credit risk in the economy factor in their expectation that, when interest rates rise, latent loan losses could emerge in banks' corporate loan books from levels that are presently exceptionally low.

Industry Business Risks: Another key factor in evaluating a country's banking industry is the banking industry's structure and regulation.

The banking industry' structure includes the:

- Number and relative size of banking institutions
- Geographic or product restrictions
- Size of bank loans in overall financial markets
- Non-bank competitors
- Depth of public capital market
- Barriers to entry
- Trends in industry
- Equity holdings or other interlocking relationships
- Political influence on bank lending decisions
- Strength and efficiency of country's legal system
- Quality and transparency of accounting

The banking industry's regulation includes:

- State, national and international regulations
- Trends in regulation
- Regulatory structure -- level & quality
- Regulatory structure - degree of independence
- Types of reporting by banks to regulators
- Regulatory authority
- Track record of regulators
- Attitude of regulators toward bank support

For example, Standard and Poor's rates the US banking industry BBB+ as well. It believes the 2010 Dodd-Frank Wall Street Reform and Consumer Protection Act is reshaping the competitive environment for banks and that a more stringent focus by US regulators on qualitative factors (for example, risk management and governance), as well as on forward-looking post-stress capital ratios, will continue to constrain banks' risk appetite. It views funding risk favorably because US banks typically benefit from a high and stable share of core deposits and exceptionally deep capital markets. Their assessment of industry business risk also considers the ongoing constraints to competitive dynamics from a sizable nonbank sector and the continued prominence of the government-sponsored entities. Economic and industry business risk combined provide the collective parameters for rating banks within a country.

Industry Risk	STANDARD & POORS' ANCHOR MATRIX									
	Economic Business Risk									
	1	2	3	4	5	6	7	8	9	10
1	a	a	a-	Bbb+	bbb+	bbb	-	-	-	-
2	a	a-	a-	bbb+	bbb	bbb	bbb-	-	-	-
3	a-	a-	bbb+	bbb+	bbb	bbb-	bbb-	bb+	-	-
4	bbb+	bbb+	bbb+	bbb	bbb	bbb-	bb+	bb	bb	-
5	bb+	bbb	bbb	bbb	bbb-	bbb-	bb+	bb	bb-	b+
6	bbb	bbb	bbb-	bbb-	bbb-	bb+	bb	bb	bb-	b+
7	-	bbb-	bbb-	bb+	bb+	bb	bb	bb-	b+	b+
8		-	bb+	bb	bb	bb	bb-	bb-	b+	b
9		-	-	bb	bb-	bb-	b+	b+	b+	b
10		-	-	-	b+	b+	b+	b	b	b-

In general, the ratings from the anchor matrix are not for the strongest individual banks in a country but for strong secondary banks. For example, in the US with an industry and economic business risk of 3 or bbb+ that would mean a half a dozen banks would have a stand-alone rating higher than BBB+, 20 to 30 of the secondary banks would have a BBB+ rating and the remainder of the banks would have a stand-alone rating of less than BBB+.

In other words, S&P's anchor for a bank operating mainly in the US is based on an economic business risk score of 3 (BBB+) and an industry business risk score of 3 (BBB+) and it would notch up and down from that anchor depending upon the individual banks' individual business and financial risk. It views the trends for both U.S. economic and industry business risk as stable.

Individual Bank Factors

Individual bank factors include individual business risks and individual financial risks.

Individual Business Factors

Individual business factors include the individual bank's market positon, the extent of its diversification and its management and strategy.

Its *market positon* includes its customer's price sensitivity, level of sophistication, relationship between banks and corporate clients, market share by product and the advantage/disadvantage of market shares and benefits/vulnerabilities of its market position. JP Morgan has the leading market positon in many areas of its business.

Its *diversity* includes the diversity of the bank's customer base, products/business lines, home markets and geography. JP Morgan derives its income from many different lines of business.

Its *management and strategy* includes an evaluation of its organizational structure, controls/information systems, performance vs. peers, credibility, succession planning, special ownership characteristics and realism, logic and risk of its strategy. JP Morgan has followed a consistent conservative management strategy over many years.

Because of its strong business position S&P notches JP Morgan's stand-alone rating up one notch from BBB+ to A-.

Individual Financial Risks

Rating agencies evaluate the following areas in assessing a bank's individual financial risk:

Credit Risk Rating	_____
Earnings Rating	_____
Liquidity and Funding Rating	_____
Market Risk Rating	_____
Capitalization Rating	_____
Financial Flexibility Rating	_____
OVERALL FINANCIAL RISK RATING	_____

The basic question of financial risks is the standard of certainty that you wish to apply. "It's a question of whether you want to insure against a 100-year flood or a 30-year flood." - *Treasury Secretary Timothy Geithner.* "A bank, or any financial intermediary, requires significant leverage to be competitive." *-Former Federal Reserve Chairman Mr. Greenspan.*

According to the OCC (Office of the Comptroller of Currency), 81% of failed banks were caused by failed credit risk management.

Rating Agency bank credit analysis looks at quality through a quantitative set of historic figures. (Balance Sheet, P&L and Cash Flow Statements and/or other data). The objective is to get "behind the figures" to look at the quality of credit risk management.

Factors that can lead to bank failure include a rapidly expanding portfolio, funding the loan book with hi-volume, volatile deposits and becoming dependent on one sector (e.g. telecoms, real estate, oil & gas, etc.).

Credit Risk Rating

The Credit risk rating is from a bank's *asset credit quality* evaluated through its *credit intrinsic risk, credit characteristics, non-performing assets, loan loss allowance and key ratios*.

Asset credit quality evaluates *intrinsic risk*, including the relative proportions of assets in different risk categories including low risk assets (e.g. government bills; interbank deposits, derivative counter party exposure) and higher risk assets (e.g. loans; equities).

Asset credit quality evaluates *credit characteristics* within risk categories such as size, maturity, currency, collateral, product concentrations and sector and borrower concentrations.

Asset credit quality evaluates *non-performing assets* that include loans not paying interest or defaulted derivative contracts, restructured loans (paying less than originally agreed and/or with extended maturity), real estate owned and loans accruing interest but that management considers problematic.

Asset credit quality evaluates the *loan loss allowance.* The loan loss allowance is a balance sheet item, usually a contra asset. For example,

- The loan loss allowance at previous year-end.
- Plus the loss provision for the current year,
- Minus the previous year's loan losses (net of recoveries),
- Equals the new loan loss allowance at year-end.

Loan loss provisions are a charge to the P&L. Like many areas in banking, there is room for judgment about the correct amount. There is a danger managements will understate losses is recessions to smooth earnings.

Asset credit quality evaluates *key ratios*. The key ratios evaluating credit risk ratings are:

- Loan loss allowance / total loan portfolio
- Loan loss allowance / latest year's charge-offs
- Loan loss provision / latest year's charge-offs

Other considerations are the structure of on and off balance sheet credit exposures including the amount and nature of fixed income securities, the amount and nature of equity securities, the nature and risk of the loan portfolio, the concentrations of the loan portfolio and the amount and nature of derivative counterparty exposure. The question is the size of problem loans, the adequacy of loan loss reserves and reserve policy.

In each of the above credit areas JP Morgan has performed better than its peers.

Earnings Rating

Rating agencies determine the earnings rating by the:

- Net Interest income: margin trends
- Non-interest income: diversity and sustainability
- Operating expenses: level and trend
- Loan loss provision: current level, volatility
- Net operating income analysis: level and trend
- Quality of earnings: core earnings vs. trading, etc.

Extraordinary gains and/or losses

Other earnings factors include the tax position, the impact of inflation on earnings, the earnings outlook, the quality of accounting practices and most importantly the earnings level relative to risk. JP Morgan has had substantially more stable earnings than its competitors.

Capitalization Rating

Capitalization: evaluates the capital composition, the capital relative to level of risk, the capital relative to domestic capital requirements, the dividend payout ratio, the absolute size of the bank's capital, the ability of the bank to raise capital and management philosophy regarding risk asset and loan leveraging.

Capitalization evaluates a bank's reliance on short-term wholesale funding that pressure net interest margins and may result in the market value depreciation in investment securities and MBS portfolios and raises questions about the traditional strategy of borrowing short and lending long.

Capitalization evaluates a bank use of securitization of assets as a means of reducing interest rate risk. This is an effective tool for capital, asset/liability management but it is not without risk. Although accounting policies allow banks to remove sold assets from the balance sheet not all risks associated with asset sales are necessarily off-loaded.

Capitalization also evaluates risks potentially retained by bank including:

- the retention of first loss on any credit losses incurred on assets in the pool,
- the possible loss of the retention of a variable income stream (excess servicing income),
- the potential loss of the customer relationship,
- the reputation risk in event of default, and
- the potential need to reconsolidate off balance sheet asset backed securities in the event of default.

JP organ has more capital relative to its risk weighted assets than its competitors

Liquidity and Funding Rating

Liquidity and funding risks evaluate the composition of a bank's funding, the diversity of its funding sources, its flows of funds, its asset liquidity and its liquidity policies. (For more information see Liquidity Risk Page 60.). JP Morgan has more stable and diverse source of liquidity that its competitors.

Market Risk Rating

In the past, US banks have increased their reliance on wholesale funds. The competition for retail deposits from nonbanking entities has led to increased usage of wholesale funds and strong loan growth has outstripped deposit growth, further pressuring liquidity profile. JP Morgan because of its large investment banking operations is subject to more market risk than its competitors.

Support Factors In Bank Ratings

Virtually all banking systems benefit from government support via regulation. There is not guarantee of timely payment of bank's financial obligations but government support does mitigate some risks. Government support is a part of the industry risk assessment; it is not an explicit factor in most bank ratings but after 2008, rating agencies and banks recognize it as being much more important!

Group Bank Rating Methodology

The group bank rating methodology provides a consistent framework for assessing the creditworthiness of the global consolidated organization as well as the individual members of the group. The methodology for group-supported ratings involves a top down analysis and a bottom-up analysis.

The three-stage approach involves the assessment of the global consolidated organization followed by a stand-alone rating of the primary operating companies based on their strategic importance. Rating agencies base the Group Rating on the consolidated or aggregated group as if it were a single corporate entity. The Group Rating is usually the same as Counterparty Credit Rating of primary operating companies. The Group Rating is reference point for ratings assigned to individual group members.

The Stand-alone Rating assesses the group member as if it were a separate entity. It removes all the positive and/or negative effects of group membership from the rating.

Rating agencies assign only a status quo rating if the group member is not viable outside of the group,

Rating agencies base the Status Quo Rating on the existing elements of group membership including common operating platform; potential funding from the group, access to distribution and shared managers but excluding any potential extraordinary capital contribution.

Stress testing and credit migration models

Rating agencies evaluate the strength of their bank internally, and for their regulators, through stress tests based on a credit migration model.

Credit migration is the possible movement from an initial (non-default) category/rating of a loan to another category, over a specified time horizon, e.g., one year, due to a credit event (upgrade, downgrade, default), that causes a change in the value of the portfolio.

Rating agencies base the credit migration model on the development of a probability distribution for the possibility of credit rating changes over the risk horizon. Rating agencies derive these probabilities from empirical observations of historical ratings and default data. The One Year Transition Rate Table below summarizes probability distribution for each rating category based on S&P ratings and transition matrices.

As can be seen from this transition matrix, any company that was rated AAA by S&P at the beginning of the year had an 87.1% likelihood that it would still be rated AAA (and therefore have the same value) by the end of the year. It would have a 9.0% likelihood that S&P would rate it AA by the end of the year (and therefore depreciate in value according to the reduced price of AA's relative to AAA's) by the end of the year. Banks complete these calculations for all loans. The severity of the stress test recession and the ratings of a Bank's loans will determine if a Bank has sufficient capital to absorb losses from its portfolio of loans and pass the stress test.

S&P Normal Global Corporate Average One-Year Transition Rates

	RATING AT YEAR-END %							
	AAA	AA	A	BBB	BB	B	CCC	D
AAA	87.1	9.0	0.5	0.1	0.1	0.0	0.0	0.00
AA	0.5	86.7	8.1	0.5	0.1	0.0	0.0	0.0
A	0.03	1.8	87.7	5.4	0.3	0.1	0.0	0.0
BBB	0.0	0.1	3.6	85.4	3.8	0.5	0.1	0.2
BB	0.0	0.0	0.1	5.1	76.8	7.0	0.6	1.4
B	0.0	0.0	0.1	0.2	5.3	74,3	4.4	3,8
CCC	0.0	0.0	0.1	0.2	0.6	12.8	44.9	26.4

Banks base the transition matrix on default ratings. Banks adjusts the estimated declines in value based on risk mitigation techniques. These mitigation techniques include collateralization, asset securitization, netting, guarantees, letters of credit and hedging.

Collateralization includes pledge liquid assets in a mark-to-market arrangement based on previously agreed ratings change thresholds.

Asset securitization includes collateralized debt obligations (CDOs) collateralized by pools of bank loans or corporate bonds. The asset securitization process allows a bond/loan portfolio to be bundled into different risk classes with ratings gradations that can appeal to different investor classes. Banks frequently issue CDOs as an arbitrage of regulatory capital requirements. In other words, by securitizing assets, banks no longer have to maintain capital to support them and this frees up capital for additional loans.

Netting includes offsetting of positive and negative derivative mark-to-market gains and losses in determination of the credit- equivalent amount for capital requirements. Netting requires a legal bilateral netting agreement with a single counterparty.

Guarantees include fee-based commitments from an insurer with a higher credit rating than the insured that guarantees the obligations of the insured.

Letters of Credit include commitments issued by a financial institution, for a fee, that provide for a payment to the buyer of the letter of credit in the event of a future event such as a default.

Credit Derivatives include commitments from a counterparty, such as credit default swaps and other structured products, to pay principle to the purchaser of the credit derivative in return for the bond/loan in the event of a default.

Operational Risk Management

Operational Risk includes the possibility of loss arising from failures in people, systems, processes and adverse external events.

Internal sources of operational risk include transaction errors, criminal activity (internal theft, fraud), inadequate controls, technological/system failure and regulatory/fiduciary violations. External Sources: of operational risk include strategic errors, criminal activity (external theft, fraud), catastrophic natural events, technological/system failure and regulatory changes.

Operational Risk is significant because of the potential magnitude of operational risk exposures, the difficulty of identifying and quantifying operational risk exposures, the overlap with and/or interdependence with credit, market and other risks and the difficulty of "hedging" or managing operational risks.

The essentials of operational risk management include the identification, assessment, monitoring, control and mitigation of operational risk. Operational Risk Management is not new. Banks have traditionally focused on the prevention of specific operational losses. However, there is now an acknowledgement of operational risk as a risk class deserving of the same management attention and treatment as market and credit risk. There is now an attempted application of a comprehensive, systematic analytical approach to risk measurement and management that results in "Sound Practices".

These sound practices include the development of an appropriate risk management environment including board awareness of and approval for an operating risk management framework and requirement for independent internal operating risk management audits. The sound practices also include senior management responsibility for implementation of the operating risk management framework including its policies, processes, procedures and systems. The sound practices develop appropriate risk management procedures including risk identification of internal and external potential adverse events, risk assessment of the likelihood of adverse events, risk control that accepts, mitigates, or eliminates operational risks, risk monitoring - for timely detection and remedy and contingency planning to ensure a timely business recovery.

Integrated Risk Management

The objective of bank risk management is to develop a comprehensive and coordinated framework of policies, infrastructure and processes for identifying, measuring, assessing and managing risks at the enterprise level. There are many risks facing a bank including credit risks, market risks, operational risks, interest rate risks, liquidity risks, settlement risks, legal risks, reputational risks and sovereign risks.

Bank risk management has evolved through increasingly sophisticated methods of risk identification, measurement, monitoring and controlling. It has also evolved through methods of integrating risk evaluation with capital management.

The driving factors behind this sophistication and integration are the complexity and interdependence of risks affecting the firm, the legislation permitting consolidation in the financial services sector and the business and regulatory need to address all risks facing the firm.

The factors that have enabled this increased sophistication include increased shareholder emphasis on the value of risk management, improving financial engineering systems and information technology and regulatory incentives. Risk management trends include the desire to manage limits by risk class, by value-at-risk amounts, by capital and by shareholder value. These risk management trends have resulted in risk management frameworks that result in risk policies, technological systems, process infrastructures and VaR, stress testing and portfolio optimization methodologies.

They have also resulted in changed risk management roles and responsibilities. The roles and responsibilities of the _Board of Directors_ include the development of risk management philosophies and policies, the establishment of risk tolerance and limits of organization and the definition of lines of authority.

The roles and responsibilities of the _Senior Management_ includes the development and implementation of procedures for management of risk creating businesses and support groups. These procedures include the allocation of risk limits down to business units, the provision of risk measurement and monitoring systems, the establishment of risk reporting against limits, the review of exposures vs. limits and the regular review of risk management methods and models.

The roles and responsibilities of the _Independent Risk Management_ function include the measurement of valuation models such as VaR, stress testing, portfolio and capital management models, the limit process, the monitoring and reporting risk against limits and limit exceptions monitoring and reporting.

The roles and responsibilities of the _Operations_ function include the booking, settlement & reconciliation of trades and positions, the independent mark-to-market and daily profit and loss.

The roles and responsibilities of the _Internal Audit_ function include the separation of duties, the assessment of internal risk management controls, the assessment of the risk management information system and the compliance with risk management policies.

The roles and responsibilities of the _Finance_ function include the assessment and validation of the profit and loss integrity.

Economic Capital Management: The primary function of capital is to act as a cushion to absorb unanticipated losses. Banks calculate their risk-based capital ratio by dividing their qualifying capital (the numerator of the ratio) by their risk-weighted assets (the denominator). Economic capital is the capital necessary to absorb unanticipated, or unexpected, losses at a specified level of confidence.

Banks expect their loan loss reserves to absorb anticipated, or expected, losses. _Expected loss_ is the provision for loan loss. A banks' provision for loan losses is an expense item in the income statement.

The objective of the Risk Adjusted Return on Capital (RAROC) is to relate the return on capital on a transaction or business to the risk/reward preferences of the organization. RAROC integrates the risk/reward preferences of the shareholders and the organization into its pricing and capital management policies and procedures.

Economic capital is risk-adjusted capital. VaR is the model used to calculate economic capital. The level of confidence is a business decision, reflecting the amount of risk acceptable to senior management and shareholders.

$$\text{RAROC} = \text{Risk Adjusted Return/Risk adjusted Capital}$$
$$= \text{Net Revenue - Expected loss/Economic capital}$$

Risk-Adjusted Return is gross revenue consisting of spread, fees and equity credit <u>*minus*</u> operating expenses (including the expected loss) or net income before taxes minus taxes equals net income after tax or the Risk Adjusted Return.

Risk-Adjusted Capital is the Exposure (expected loss as a percent of anticipated exposure at default)

  x Stand-alone standard deviation
  x Risk Contribution (From Model Based Var-Covar Matrix)
    = Net Risk Contribution to Portfolio
  x Capital Factor
    = Economic Capital or Risk Adjusted Capital

The Return on Risk Adjusted Capital is equal to the risk adjusted return/risk adjusted capital. Therefore, banks design economic capital to absorb "unexpected losses".

What Went Wrong?

What went wrong in 2007-2008 with all these sophisticated risk measurement calculations? As Aristotle said, "Never try to bring any greater precision to a subject matter than the nature of the subject matter permits." These Modem Portfolio Management methodologies resulted in extremely complicated formulas that implied a greater precision in managing capital that the inputs (particularly the rating systems) permitted.

For example, as mentioned earlier, for residential mortgage backed securities originally rated AAA from 2005 to 2007 by Standard & Poor's only:

Remained AAA	33.1%
Downgrades to Other A Ratings	6.1%
Downgrades to B Ratings	19.1%
Downgrades to C Ratings	39.3%
Downgrades to D Ratings	<u>2.4%</u>
TOTAL	100.0%

This is hardly an acceptable estimate of credit quality based on historical expectations from prior year's ratings of 88.1% of AAA's remaining AAA over that time.

Chapter: 6
Derivative Credit Analysis

The objective of this chapter is to explain derivatives and evaluate derivative credit risk. The objective is to clarify how to construct derivative cash flows, explain the objectives of derivative activities, describe how to analyze financial statements to evaluate a bank's market risk from derivative activities and how to integrate this assessment into an overall assessment of a Bank's credit risk.

Background on Derivatives

A derivative is a _financial contract_ between two parties (called counter parties). The contract deals with _future payments._ The contract sets _dates for the payments._ The amount of a payment is based on or will be based on (or derived from) some _underlying._ The _underlying_ can be a reference rate, price or index. Traders multiply the _underlying_ by the _notional amount_ of the contract to determine one or both of the payment amounts. The value of a derivative, therefore, depends on (varies with) the value of the _underlying._

Derivative underlyings include:

- _interest rates_ such as the London Interbank Offering Rate (LIBOR), commercial paper, treasury bills;
- _exchange rates_ such as the Canadian $/US$, Japanese ¥/US$, US$/UK£;
- _commodity prices_ such as the price of gold, wheat, oil; and
- _stock indexes_ such as the S&P 500, or the NYSE

The key derivative notional amounts are _currencies_ such as the US$, Can$, €, £, ¥, _commodities_ such as bushels, tons, lbs. and _stocks_ such as IBM, GM, ATT.

There are two generic types of derivatives. A derivative contract either _requires_ an exchange of future payments (a FORWARD contract) or a derivative contract grants one party the _option to require_ an exchange of future payments (an OPTION contract).

Simple derivative forwards and their complex products include:

Forwards	Simple Forward	Complex Product
Interest Rate	Forward Rate Agreements	Interest Rate Swaps
Currency	Forward Foreign Exchange	Currency Swaps
Commodity	Commodity Forwards	Commodity Swaps
Stock Index	Stock Index Forwards	Stock Index Forwards
Credit Rating	Default Swaps	Total Return Swaps

Simple derivative options and their complex products include

Options	Simple Option	Complex Product
Interest Rate	Interest Rate Option	Caps, Collars & Floors
Currency	Foreign Exchange Option	N. A.
Commodity	Commodity Options	Commodity Swap Options
Stock Index	Stock Index Option	Stock Index Swap Options
Credit Rating	Default Swap Options	Total Return Swap Options

Interest Rate Swaps consist of a series of exchanges of future interest payments. Each individual exchange consists of a FRA - a forward rate agreement

FRA #1	FRA #2	FRA #3	FRA #4
Period 1	Period 2	Period 3	Period 4
Fixed	Fixed	Fixed	Fixed
↓	↓↑	↓↑	↓↑
	Variable	Variable	Variable	Variable

Derivative Credit Exposure is the potential cost that one party would have to pay to replace a contract with another counterparty at a particular point in time if the other party should go bankrupt.

Mark-to-market gains are the profits an entity would make if outstanding derivatives were sold (or closed out) at current market prices. *Mark-to-market losses* are the losses an entity would make if outstanding derivatives were sold (or closed out) at current market prices.

Mark-to-market exposure of Derivative Products 3/31/16

Forwards		
	Foreign Exchange Forwards	45%
	Currency Swaps	20%
	Interest Rate Swaps	15%
Options		
	Foreign Exchange Options	10%
Other Derivative Products		<u>10%</u>
TOTAL		100%

A *foreign exchange forward* requires one counterparty to buy, and the other to sell, a currency, at a specific exchange rate (the *underlying*) in a specific amount (the *notional amount*) on a specific date in the future (the *settlement date*).

A *foreign exchange option* contract gives the option holder the right, *but not the obligation* to buy or sell a *notional amount* of foreign exchange at a price, called the strike price, *(the underlying)* during a period or on a specific date.

Exercise1: Questions
Identifying Derivatives

Which of the following are derivatives? If a derivative, what type? Please explain.

1. On January 1, 2016, A agrees to pay 6-month LIBOR to B on 100 million US$, payment to be made on June 30, 2016 and Dec. 31, 2016. B agrees to pay A 6% on 100 million US$, on Dec. 31, 2016.

2. On February 1, 2016, A signs a contract for $2 million with B to build an office building. The office building is to be completed, and payment to be made, on Dec. 31, 2016.

3.   On January 15, 2016, A agrees to sell his house to B for $200,000 with a closing date on Feb. 28, 2016.

4.   On January 1, 2016, A agrees to give B, as collateral, $105 million in US government agency structured notes, and B agrees to lend A $100 million. Simultaneously, A agrees to buy back the $105 million in US government agency structured notes in 30 days, for $100 million, plus accrued interest, at the 30-day repo rate. Interest on the government agency structured note accrues to A and varies with the 180-day T-bill rate.

Exercise 1: Answers
Identifying Derivatives

Which of the following are derivatives? If a derivative, what type? Please explain.

1.   On January 1, 2016, A agrees to pay 6-month LIBOR to B on 100 million US$, payment to be made on June 30, 2016 and Dec. 31, 2016. B agrees to pay A 6% on 100 million US$, on Dec. 31, 2016.

Yes, this is a derivative. It is an interest rate swap contract traded over the counter. The contract meets all the criteria of a derivative.

2.   On February 1, 008, A signs a contract for $2 million with B to build an office building. The office building is to be completed, and payment to be made, on Dec. 31, 2016.

No, this is not a derivative. It is a construction contract. The contract is not a derivative. Its value is not based on a "benchmark."

3.   On January 15, 2016, A agrees to sell his house to B for $200,000 with a closing date on Feb. 28, 2016.

No, this is not a derivative. It is a future sale contract. The contract is not a derivative because its value is not based on a "benchmark."

4.   On January 1, 2016, A agrees to give B, as collateral, $105 million in US government agency structured notes, and B agrees to lend A $100 million. Simultaneously, A agrees to buy back the $105 million in US government agency structured notes in 30 days, for $100 million, plus accrued interest, at the 30-day repo rate. Interest on the government agency structured note accrues to A and varies with the 180-day T-bill rate.

No, this is not a derivative. It is a repurchase agreement contract. The contract is a cash secured loan contract not a future payment contract. Counterparties exchange cash at trade date for securities that one counterparty holds as collateral for the loan.

Exercise 2: Questions
Constructing Derivative Cash Flows

Please construct the cash flows for the following derivative transactions:

1. On January 1, 2016, A buys a one year $10 million Forward Rate Agreement from B and agrees to pay 6% fixed on December 31, 2016 and receive LIBOR +1/2 %. Please construct the cash flows for this transaction.

A
|_1/1_____3/31_____6/30_____9/30_____12/31_|

                                 2016

B

2. On January 1, 2015, A enters into a $100 million interest rate swap with B maturing 12/31/16. A agrees to pay 6-month LIBOR every 6 months. B agrees to pay 6% fixed at each year-end. Please construct the cash flows for this transaction.

A
1/1	3/31	6/30	9/30	12/31	1/1	3/31	6/30	9/30	12/31

      2015   2016

B

Exercise 2: Answers:
Constructing Derivative Cash Flows

Please construct the cash flows for the following derivative transactions:

1. On January 1, 2016, A buys one year $10 million Forward Rate Agreement from B and agrees to pay 6% fixed on December 31, 2016 and receive LIBOR +1/2 %. Please construct the cash flows for this transaction.

A pays 6% of $10 million or $600,000 on 12/31/2016

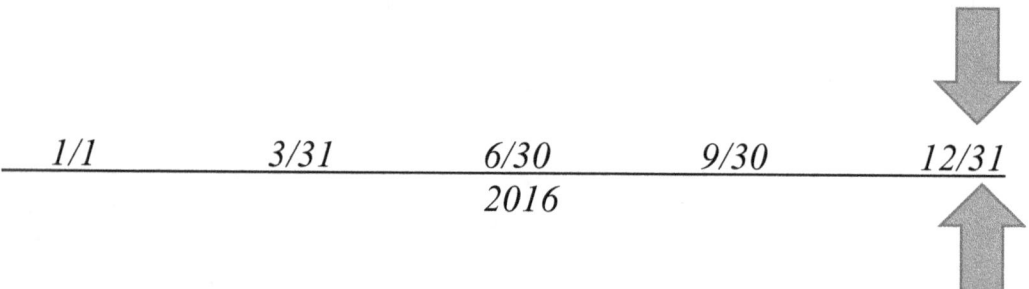

B pays 12 month LIBOR on 12/31/16 + 1/2% times $10 million

2. On January 1, 2015, A enters into a $100 million interest rate swap with B maturing 12/31/16. A agrees to pay 6-month LIBOR every 6 months. B agrees to pay 6% fixed at each year-end. Please construct the cash flows for this transaction.

```
    $100 mm X .5 X     $100 mm X .5 X     $100 mm X .5 X     $100 mm X .5
    6 Month LIBOR      6 month LIBOR      6 month LIBOR      X 6 month LIBOR

         ↓                  ↓                  ↓                  ↓

  1/1  3/31   6/30   9/30   12/31   3/31   6/30   9/30   12/31
                    2015                        2016

                          ↑                              ↑

    B Pays            $6 million                     $6 million
```

Daily Derivative Volume

	Foreign Exchange	Swaps	FX Options
$ Billions	$1,500	$28	$400
Daily # of Transactions	1,500,000	2,800	200,000
Complexity	1 trade	10 trades	1 trade
Duration	.1 year	2.7 years	.1 year
Margins	.01%	.50%	.03%

In *over-the-counter derivative markets* counterparties are large clients, contracts are for individually tailored amounts and 50% of contracts are un-collateralized. The market consists of *forwards* & options.

In *exchange traded derivative markets* counterparties are small retail clients, contracts are for standardized amounts, terms and maturities, and exchanges collateralize 100% of the contracts. The market consists of *futures* & options

The disadvantages of exchange traded contracts is that it is difficult to tailor a contract to meet specific needs, the market is ineffective for large hedging needs and collateralization may require calls for additional funds.

Benefits of Derivatives

Derivatives provide benefits to purchaser through comparative advantage or financing cost reduction, through trading, spreads within a market, through arbitrage, or spreads between markets, through hedging or financial insurance and through partially hedged or unhedged positions or speculation.

Cost Reduction: Derivative products may be used to *reduce costs* for a purchaser by capitalizing on the advantage one counterparty holds in one market compared to the relative advantage another counterparty holds in another market.

For example, high yield credits, like cyclical credits, generally already have significant business risk and therefore wish to reduce financial risk (interest rate risk) by borrowing at a fixed rate. At the same time, while banks are willing to lend at a variable rate to high yield credits they are often unwilling to lend at a fixed rate for the same reason, because it will make the credit riskier. Therefore, high yield credits have a "variable rate comparative advantage" i.e. relatively can borrow more cheaply at a variable rate than at a fixed rate.

On the other hand, A or better credits like branded consumer product companies, normally have low business risk and can borrow relatively attractively at long term fixed rates. They can take on the added financial risk (interest rate risk) of borrowing at variable rates because their business risk is so low. At the same time if they were to borrow at variable rates, their variable rate relatively would not be that much better than that of a high yield credit. Therefore A or better credits have a "fixed rate comparative advantage" i.e. relatively can borrow more cheaply at fixed rates than at fixed rates.

It makes no difference that, in absolute terms, the A or better credit can borrow more cheaply at both fixed and variable rates than the high yield credit. They both can benefit by borrowing at their comparative advantage rate and through an interest rate swap, swap into the rate they prefer at a reduced cost.

Trading: Traders can buy and sell derivative products to *make money* by acting as an intermediary between different clients *within markets.* The spread is the difference between the traders buy and the sell price.

Arbitrage: Traders can buy and sell derivative products to make money by exploiting inconsistencies *between different markets* at a given point in time. For example, they can buy an equity in New York and sell it in Tokyo.

Hedging: Companies use derivative products as a form of financial insurance to reduce vulnerability to interest rate, currency, and commodity and security price volatility. There are two basic types of hedging activity: hedges to protect against volatility of existing assets and liabilities (fair value hedges) and hedges to protect against volatility of anticipated cash flows (cash flow hedges).

An example of when interest rate hedging would have been helpful occurred in 1980 in the Savings and Loan Industry. Savings and Loan banks *Received Fixed* on the 30 Year Fixed Rate Mortgage Loans they made to their customers. However, they funded these loans by *Paying Variable* on Short Term Certificates Of Deposit to their retail customers. When short-term interest rates increased dramatically under Federal Reserve Chairman Paul Volker, these dramatically increased funding costs caused enormous losses.

Speculation: Traders and companies can buy and sell derivatives, and leave them unhedged or partially hedged to capitalize on market moves by removing the restraint on potential positive moves.

Derivative Credit Exposure Pricing: Traders calculate pricing for derivatives using the Value-at-Risk (VaR) methodology. Traders use VaR to calculate the average expected exposure and then multiply that amount by the expected default cost of the counterparty based on the counterparty's credit rating and the historical default experience for those ratings over a comparable time.

Default Bond Recovery Prices as percentage of Par 1974-2006

Type of structure	Discounted % of par value at Emergence
Senior Secured	64
Senior Unsecured	50
Senior Subordinated	28
Junior Subordinated	13
All Instruments	51

Traders usually only trade derivatives with investment grade credits on an unsecured basis. Traders usually collateralize non-investment grade derivative credit exposure. The reason for this is that although courts in bankruptcy regard derivative credit exposure as senior unsecured exposure, unsecured derivative counterparties usually lack the ability to call for collateral that is available to other senior unsecured debt like bank debt. As a result, when there are defaults and credit exposure is uncollateralized, recoveries are lower than for other senior debt.

Product	M-T-M as a % of Notional	Notional to M-T-M
Interest Rate Swap	1.0%	100 times
Currency Swap	5.0%	20 times
FX Forwards	2.0%	50 times
FX Options	2.0%	50 times
FRA's	0.5%	200 times

Derivative Credit Exposure Management

Trader measurement of derivative credit risk is complicated by the fact that notional reporting of derivative credit exposure is not meaningful. For example, for interest rate swaps notional reporting overstates historical average of mark-to-market credit exposures by 100 times and for currency swaps by 20 times.

Current Exposure Measurement: The advantages of "current Exposure" or "mark-to-market exposure" is that it can be calculated easily and precisely and can be added to or subtracted from any other type of exposure. The disadvantage of "Current Exposure" is that it can understate credit exposure since it takes no account of future potential exposure. (For example, at trade date there is no "Current Exposure' since counterparties execute the trade at market price.)

Average & Peak Expected Exposures: Traders calculate "Average Expected Exposure" on the average of all historical credit exposures over a specific time. "Peak Expected Exposure" is based on the extremes of historical variations in credit exposures which happen only once out of twenty days (or once out of 100 days) over a specific time.

Average Expected Volatility: Average expected exposure is calculated by first calculating average expected volatility. The example below uses a hypothetical yen/dollar exchange rate and volatility over a 20 business day period.

Average Expected Volatility

Day #	¥/$ Exchange	Volatility %	Day #	¥/$ Exchange	Volatility %
0	100.0				
1	100.2	+.2	11	99.4	-.7
2	99.7	-.5	12	99.9	+.5
3	100.1	+.4	13	100.1	+.2
4	99.9	-.2	14	100.7	+.6
5	100.3	+.4	15	100.4	-.3
6	100.8	+.5	16	100.1	-.3
7	100.2	-.6	17	100.4	+.3
8	100.9	+.7	18	100.2	-.2
9	100.5	-.4	19	100.5	+.3
10	100.1	-.4	20	100.0	-.5
Total				2,000.0	8.0
	Average	Expected	Volatility	8/2,000 =	.4%

Traders calculate *average expected volatility* by listing the percent change in exchange rates for each day of a designated period. Traders them total all percent changes (whether plus or minus and divide the total percent change by the number of days to arrive at the average daily expected volatility.

Peak expected volatility: Traders calculate the peak expected volatility by listing the percent change in exchange rates in order of size on each day and select the nineteenth highest positive daily percent change in the 20-day period (or 100-day period).

Peak Expected Volatility

Day #	Volatility %	Day #	Volatility %	By size	By Size
0	—			—	
1	+.2	11	-.7	-.7	+.2
2	-.5	12	+.5	-.6	+.2
3	+.4	13	+.2	-.5	+.3
4	-.2	14	+.6	-.5	+.3
5	+.4	15	-.3	-.4	+.4
6	+.5	16	-.3	-.4	+.4
7	-.6	17	+.3	-.3	+.5
8	+.7	18	-.2	-.3	+.5
9	-.4	19	+.3	-.2	**+.6**
10	-.4	20	-.5	-.2	+.7
	Peak	Expected	Volatility		**.6%**

Average Expected Exposure: Traders take the percent change in exchange rates for each day, total all positive percent changes, and then divide the total positive percent changes by the number of days to arrive at the average expected exposure per day. Only positive exposures are counted as exposures because negative exposure are losses. If you have a loss you will still have to pay the bankruptcy court the same amount.

Average Expected Exposure

Day #	¥/$ Exchange	Gains %	Day#	¥/$ Exchange	Gains %
0	100.0				
1	100.2	+.2	11	99.4	
2	99.7	0	12	99.9	+.5
3	100.1	+.4	13	100.1	+.2
4	99.9	0	14	100.7	+.6
5	100.3	+.4	15	100.4	
6	100.8	+.5	16	100.1	
7	100.2	0	17	100.4	+.3
8	100.9	+.7	18	100.2	
9	100.5	0	19	100.5	+.3
10	100.1	0	20	100.0	
Total				2,000.0	4.0
	Average	Expected	Exposure	4/2,000 =	.2%

Peak Expected Exposure: To calculate the Peak Credit exposure traders take the credit exposure for each day of a designated period in order of size, and select the 19th largest credit exposure for per 20-day period.

Peak Expected Exposure

Day #	Volatility %	Day #	Volatility %	By size	By Size
0	—			—	
1	+.2	11	-.7	0	+.2
2	-.5	12	+.5	0	+.2
3	+.4	13	+.2	0	+.3
4	-.2	14	+.6	0	+.3
5	+.4	15	-.3	0	+.4
6	+.5	16	-.3	0	+.4
7	-.6	17	+.3	0	+.5
8	+.7	18	-.2	0	+.5
9	-.4	19	+.3	0	**+.6**
10	-.4	20	-.5	0	+.7
	Peak	Expected	Exposure		.6%

A key assumption of VaR is that it assumes a normal distribution of events. Normal distributions simply assume that the daily variability of events is simply the square root of the number of days. Therefore, to calculate the average expected exposure over different times one merely multiplies the 1-day volatility by the square root of the number of days to obtain the expected exposure over different times. For example, traders assume the average expected exposure for a two-day trade is merely the volatility of a one-day trade times the square root of two.

Average Expected Exposure Maturity Bands

Notional Amount	Day	Average Expected Volatility	1 Day Average Exposure	Average Expected Exposure
$10 MM	1	.2		$20,000
	2	Square Root of 2 or 1.414	$20,000	$28,280
	3	Square Root of 3 or 1.732	$20,000	$34,640
	4	Square Root of 4 or 2	$20,000	$40,000
	5	Square Root of 5 or 2.236	$20,000	$44,720
	Day 1	Day 2	Day 3	Day 4
Avg. Exp. Exposure	$20,000	$28,280	$34,640	$40,000

Similarly, to calculate the peak expected exposure over different times one merely multiplies the 1-day volatility by the square root of the number of days to obtain the peak expected exposure over different times. For example, traders assume the peak exposure for a two-day trade is merely the volatility of a one-day trade times the square root of two.

Peak Expected Exposure Maturity Bands

Notional Amount	Day	Peak Expected Volatility	1 Day Peak Exposure	Peak Exp. Exposure	
$10 MM	1	.6		$60,000	
	2	Square Root of 2 or 1.414	$60,000	$84,850	
	3	Square Root of 3 or 1.732	$60,000	$103,900	
	4	Square Root of 4 or 2	$60,000	$120,000	
	5	Square Root of 5 or 2.236	$60,000	$134,200	
	Day 1	Day 2	Day 3	Day 4	Day 5
Peak Exp. Exposure	$60,000	$84,850	$103,900	$120,000	$134,200

Different derivatives have different exposures over the life of the contracts. Because there is an exchange of principle at the end of the contract, foreign exchange contracts continue to increase in exposure over the life of the contract. In contrast, because there is not an exchange of principle - only payments of interest — interest rate swaps gradually increase in exposure until half way through the contract and then gradually decline.

Furthermore, different derivatives have different variability in exposure because of their different terms. For example, portfolios of swaps that have initial average maturity of about three years vary by market moves over a year and a half. In contrast, markets affect bank portfolios of foreign exchange contracts that have average maturity of about 4 days by market moves of only 2 days.

Volatility of Portfolio Exposure

Product	M-T-M as % of Notional	Average Ratio Notional to M-T-M	Effected by Market Moves Of
Interest Rate Swap	.5% to 1.5%	200x to 70x	1 1/2 years
Currency Swap	3% to 7%	33x to 15x	1 1/2 years
Foreign Exchange	1% to 3%	100x to 33x	2 days
FX Options	1% to 3%	100x to 33x	30 days
Forward Rate Agreements	.4% to .7%	300x to 150x	30 days

In contrast, the volatility of exposure for a single contract can be much greater.

Volatility of Individual Counterparty Exposure

Product	M-T-M as % of Notional	Average Ratio Notional to M-T-M	Effected by Market Moves Of
Interest Rate Swap	+3% to -3%	+3 Ox to -3 Ox	1 1/2 years
Currency Swap	+15% to -15%	+8x to -8x	1 1/2 years
Foreign Exchange	+6% to -6%	+16x to -16x	2 days
FX Options	+6% to -6%	+16x to -16x	30 days
Forward Rate Agreements	+1.5% to -1.5%	+70x to -70x	30 days

The potential variability of exposure to an individual counterparty is one of the reasons why most uncollateralized trades are with investment grade credits where there is less worry about the possibility of default.

Risk Equivalents & Comparing Credit Exposures

Year#	AAA	AA	A	BBB	BB	B	CCC/C
1	0.00	0.02	0.07	**0.21**	0.76	3.88	26.38
2	0.03	0.07	0.16	0.57	2.35	8.80	35.58
3	0.14	0.13	0.27	0.98	4.23	12.97	40.67
4	0.24	0.24	0.41	1.46	6.06	16.22	43.77
5	0.36	0.35	0.57	1.95	7.71	18.70	46.28
10	0.74	0.82	1.51	4.06	13.74	25.91	50.73
15	0.98	1.19	2.32	5.84	16.77	29.49	53.38

Risk Equivalents compare all exposures relative to 1-year BBB credit exposure. They express any exposure in dollar terms relative the expected default cost for a $1 BBB unsecured credit exposure. The table **below shows the average cumulative default rates by rating and term. S&P Corporate Default Risk by Rating***

Thus, on the table below, all default costs as a percent of the .21% annual default cost of a 1-year BBB loan are as follows:

Risk Equivalent
15 Year Avg. Cumulative Default Rates
1981-2015 (Standard & Poor's Ratings)

(Default Costs Divided by BBB 1-year Default Cost of .21 basis points)

Year#	AAA	AA	A	BBB	BB	B
1	0.00	0.10	0.33	**1.00**	3.81	19.57
2	0.14	0.33	0.81	2.86	10.80	44.14
3	0.62	0.62	1.33	4.86	21.00	64.81
4	1.14	1.14	2.05	7.29	29.95	80.90
5	1.67	1.71	2.86	9.81	38.10	93.10
10	3.52	4.00	7.57	20.62	68.52	128.43
15	4.71	5.90	11.67	29.86	84.00	14671

As can be seen from the above table, a 1-year exposure to an A rated credit is one-third the risk of a 1-year exposure to a BBB rated credit and a BB credit exposure is almost 4 times the risk of a 1-year BBB credit exposure. Similarly, a 10-year credit exposure to a BBB is roughly three times the risk of a 10-year credit exposure to an A and less than one- third the risk of 10-year credit exposure to a BB.

Derivative Documentation: Derivative Documentation consists of oral, electronic, or written evidence that a derivative transaction has occurred. The value of derivative documentation is that it reduces BIS capital requirements, improves capital ratios, reduces balance sheet liabilities, and reduces systemic risk. According to the OCC, in 2015, netting reduced derivative current credit exposure for U.S. banks by 84%.

Settlement Risk: Settlement risk is the risk that arises when, owing to differences in time zones, one party to a transaction is required to pay the other, prior to receiving payment. Settlement Netting offsets two or more buy and sell payments, *in the same currency at the same location*, that counterparties pay to one another *on the same day*.

Closeout Netting: Closeout Netting, also known as Cross Product Close-Out Netting, is the netting permitted under ISDA and other netting agreements that permits a non-defaulting counterparty to net the gains and losses owing to and from a defaulting counterparty.

Standardized Netting Agreements: The International Swap and Derivatives Association Agreement (ISDA) provides standardized netting agreements that permit liquidation of transactions in event of default and closeout netting both within and across products. Using the agreements permits companies to obtain favored accounting treatment.

Collateralized Derivative Agreements: Collateralized derivative agreements call for additional collateral when exposure exceeds threshold amounts and permit close out netting. Using these agreements also permits companies to obtain favored accounting treatment.

FASB Reporting: Price risk generates FASB attention because price risk is a factor over which a company has no direct control and, to protect itself a company may utilize derivatives. Therefore, the use of derivatives is an activity that is symptomatic of a company's potential vulnerability to price risk.

The objective of FASB derivative reporting requirements is to clarify a company's vulnerability to the transaction price risk and the general business price risk of an underlying commodity, interest rate, exchange rate, equity index, etc.

Prior to the adoption of SFAS 133 companies generally did not record derivatives used for hedging purposes on the balance sheet. In very simple terms, FASB 133 now requires that all derivatives, whether designated for hedging or not, be recorded on the balance sheet at fair value.

The key reasons for SFAS 133 are that derivative instruments represent rights or obligations that meet the definition of financial assets. Fair value is the most relevant measure for financial assets. Companies should not report non-financial assets or liabilities, like future cash flows, on financial statements. Derivatives used for hedging should require special supporting accounting justification.

SFAS 133 covers three types of hedges — Fair Value Hedges, Cash Flow Hedges and Foreign Currency Exposure Hedges

SFAS 133-Fair Value Hedges: If a company designates a hedge as a *fair value hedge*, all changes in the fair value of the derivative and changes in the fair value of the hedged asset or liability are recognized on the balance sheet. Only the difference or the ineffective portion of the hedge affects net earnings.

SFAS 133 - Cash Flow Hedges: If a company designates a derivative as a *cash flow hedge*, the company recognizes only the effective portion of the change in the fair value of the derivative on the balance sheet. Since the company expects the offset to the hedge to come from future variable cash flows, the company also records the change in the value of the derivative as an adjustment to *other comprehensive income*. The company recognizes an adjustment to *other comprehensive income* in the income statement when the hedged item affects earning and the derivative matures. The company immediately recognizes in earning the ineffective portion of cash flow hedges.

Foreign Currency exposure Hedges: A foreign currency exposure hedge is a hedge of a net investment in a foreign operation, a foreign currency-denominated unrecognized firm commitment or a forecasted transaction. For foreign currency exposure hedges, companies report the gain or loss in other comprehensive income (outside earnings) as part of the cumulative foreign currency translation adjustment.

Derivatives used as hedges must be highly effective at reducing the risk (i.e. >80% correlation). A company must designate each derivative as a hedge, with documentation of the risk management objective and strategy for the hedge. The company must assess and explain the hedged time, the risk exposure, and effectiveness prospectively and retrospectively. On initial application, companies had to identify hedging relationships and designate anew any outstanding derivatives and document them if they were to be included as a derivative designated for hedging. Because of these onerous accounting requirements, many banks, including JP Morgan do not use hedge accounting for most of their derivative transactions.

BIS Reporting: BIS (Bank for International Settlements) reporting is a process for determining capital requirements for all bank credit exposure, including derivatives.

Regulators were concerned that participants might not sufficiently understand the risk of derivatives, were not allocating sufficient capital to cover the risks and were not properly monitoring derivative credit and derivative market exposures.

The Initial BIS 3-Step Approach: BIS based the Initial BIS 8% Capital Requirement on the notional amount of the derivative converted into a *"credit risk equivalent"*. The "credit risk equivalent" was then weighted by a factor ranging from 0-50%, called a *"counterparty risk weighting*. Finally, the counterparty *"adjusted credit risk equivalent* produced a risk-weighted asset against which banks apply the 8% *BIS capital requirement* to determine the level of capital they must hold against derivatives.

"Maturity" and "Potential future Exposure Factors"

Maturity	Potential Future Exp. Factor	Potential Future Exp. Factor	Potential Future Exp. Factor
Remaining Maturity	Interest Rate Contracts	Currency Exchange Contracts	Basis Swaps
< 1 year	0.0%	1.0%	0.0%
> 1 year	0.5%	5.0%	0.0%

Counterparty Risk Weightings: Counterparty risk weightings were:

    0% — OECD Central Governments
    10% — Public sector entities located in the same country as the bank in question
    20% — OECD Banks
    50% — All other Counterparties (including corporations, non-bank financial institutions and non-OECD banks.

Derivative Credit Loss Experience: Derivative credit loss experience has been much less than the commercial bank credit loss experience (1984-2015) for loans.

    Derivative Credit Losses (annualized)   .13%
    Average Bank Loan Credit Charge Offs   1.00%

Credit Derivatives

Credit derivatives are financial instruments whose value is derived from the credit risk associated with the debt of a third-party issuer (the reference entity) and which allow one party (the protection purchaser) to transfer that risk to another party (the protection seller). Credit derivatives expose the protection purchaser to the creditworthiness of the protection seller, as the protection seller is required to make payments under the contract when the reference entity experiences a credit event, such as a bankruptcy, a failure to pay its obligation or a restructuring.

The seller of credit protection receives a premium for providing protection but has the risk that the underlying instrument referenced in the contract will be subject to a credit event.

A Credit Derivative is an off-balance-sheet financial instrument that permits one party (the "beneficiary") to transfer the credit risk of a "reference asset," which it typically owns, to another party (the "guarantor") without actually selling the asset. Therefore, credit derivatives allow users to "un-bundle" credit risk from financial instruments and trade it separately. They payoff on the occurrence of a credit event or default and their value is based on the credit quality or credit risk of a specific issuer. Like all derivatives, traders use credit derivatives to create risk, reduce risk, or enhance yield.

The normal method of hedging credit derivatives is with an offsetting trade. However, Value-at-Risk portfolio analytics give credit to imperfect correlations as well. For example, traders estimate that if the credit derivative is fully offset the transactions do not correlate with one another and have a correlation of -1.0. On the other hand, if the credit derivatives fully correlate with one another (are to the same counterparty) they have a correlation of +1.0.

Examples of this Value-at-Risk concept include trades fully offset (correlation of -1), partially offset (two companies in the same industry but long and short positions (correlation of +.7?), partially offset (two companies in different industries but both long positions (correlations of +.8) and the same company with both long or both short positions (correlation of +1).

The OTC (over-the-counter) global credit derivatives market was approximately $3 trillion as of March 31, 2016. About $2.9 trillion of the $3.0 trillion is in the inter-bank market. Only about $100 billion results in the transfer of risk from banks to other non-bank counterparties. This $100 billion represent only .3 percent of loan portfolios of global banks.

The credit derivative market is highly concentrated. Seventeen commercial and investment banks account for 83% or $2.4 trillion of notional amount of credit derivatives. Fifty percent are in US banks, and 50% in European institutions. Ninety percent of credit derivatives are with investment grade counterparties.

Largest Credit Derivative Dealers
12/31/2015

Bank	Total Credit Derivatives $Billions	Total Credit Derivatives $Billions
JP Morgan	$409	$409
Citi Group Inc.	$139	$139
UBS AG	$128	$128
Bank of America Corp	$107	$107
Commerzbank	$97	$97

Commercial and investment banks, insurance companies and hedge funds are active as both buyers and sellers of credit derivatives. Pension funds and money managers have also acted as counterparties to credit derivative transactions.

The three distinguishing features of credit derivatives are the transfer of the credit risk associated with a "reference" asset through contingent payments based on events of default and usually, the prices of instruments before, at and shortly after default. Reference assets that are most often traded include sovereign and corporate debt instruments or syndicated bank loans.

Credit derivatives require the periodic exchange of payments or the payment of a premium rather than the payment of fees that is customary with other off-balance-sheet credit products, such as letters of credit. Credit derivatives use the same ISDA master agreement and legal format of other derivatives contracts.

Bankers use credit derivatives for risk reduction, line credit management, balance sheet management, capital management and access to new asset types and classes.

Credit derivatives are different from other derivatives because of their lack of liquidity, vulnerability to economic cycles, reputation risk and counterparty risk. There are differing views on derivatives. For example:

Warren Buffet has called derivatives "financial instruments of mass destruction". He considered acquiring AIG that had substantial credit derivative losses. Therefore, when he is talking about derivatives he is thinking of derivatives as "credit derivatives". In fact, credit derivatives are not like other derivatives, they are credit insurance policies. They are illiquid and vulnerable to economic cycles. Because derivatives are unregulated and permit substantial leverage, they are the weakest link in a systemic crisis and amplify the panic as they did in 2008-2009 with AIG and Lehman Brothers.

Paul Volker has called derivatives "speculative financial instruments". In his view, regulators should not allow banks to engage in proprietary trading because proprietary trading is speculative in nature and inconsistent with an entity whose deposits are government guaranteed. In his view, traders focus on short-term price, while bankers focus on long-term value. Traders will by their very nature adopt a "Heads I win, tails you lose" philosophy e.g. JP Morgan and the "London Whale". Their philosophy is if I make money, I receive large bonuses. If I lose money, I keep my past bonuses and the bank or the government covers my losses. Traders with their high bonuses change the culture of a bank from a relationship-oriented bank to a transaction-oriented bank.

Jamie Dimon has said regulators should allow banks to engage in derivative activities in order to make markets for their clients because banks need to be competitive. If regulators do not allow U. S. banks to provide customer's needs they will go somewhere else. Derivatives make markets more efficient. They transfer risk from those who want to avoid risk to those who can better understand and undertake risk. Banks can manage risks so that the risks they take will be acceptable relative to their earnings and capital.

JPMorgan viewed the loss from the London Whale of $6 billion as manageable compared to JPMorgan's $20 billion annual pretax income and $180 billion shareholder's equity.

To clarify who is right and who is wrong it is necessary to understand the nature of derivatives and their differences from loans. *It is worth noting the age difference. Warren Buffet and Paul Volker are in their eighties and experienced the Great Depression. Jamie Dimon is in his 50's and never experienced the great depression.*

Since derivatives are not transparent, there is a danger shareholders, regulators, rating agencies and the public will not understand their risks. Therefore, JP Morgan's fundamental approach to derivatives is to explain them in simple loan language. For JP Morgan there was always the fear that competitors would not understand derivative risks and that they would create a negative attitude toward derivatives such as actually occurred later in AIG and Lehman Brothers. The reason for this fear is that derivatives are important to JPMorgan. They account for almost 20% of pretax income and provide an important entree to clients.

While account officers can look at loan exposures individually, they must look at derivative exposures collectively. Loan exposure is arithmetic i.e. based on notional amounts. Derivative exposure is algebraic i.e. based on probabilities. Additional loans always increase exposure. Additional derivative trades sometimes can reduce exposure.

Loan exposure is value sensitive. Accountants base loan exposure on discounted cash flow and accrual accounting. Actual losses occur only upon foreclosure or liquidation. Estimated losses occur through the loan loss provisions and are judgmental. Loans result in long-term focus on value.

Derivative exposure is price sensitive. Accountants base derivative exposure on market prices and mark-to-market accounting. Traders record actual losses immediately based on market prices. Derivatives result in a short-term focus on price.

Studies of derivative "current valuation adjustments - the "CVA" — have shown that derivative market prices are approximately three times more volatile than long term loan cash flow values.

Banks allocate capital for *loans* based on notional amounts based on their creditworthiness. The long-term value approach of loan officers takes into account long term economic cycles. Loan officers look for long-term relationships with value clients with cash flow repayment over several years.

Banks allocate capital for *derivatives* on value-at-risk amounts i.e. the volatility of market prices of the derivatives over the past year. The short-term price approach of traders ignores long-term economic cycles. Traders look for transaction clients under the assumption that they can close out positons over 24 hours.

The differences are particularly acute for credit derivatives. Economic cycles affect credit derivatives over 5-10 years and volatility over the past year does not capture their true volatility. For example, real estate derivatives are affected by 50-80 year economic cycles (the Kondratieff cycle) and volatility over the past year for real estate is misleading.

Derivatives assume liquid markets and a normal distribution of prices. Since credit default swaps do not have an equal upside and downside potential return VaR is an inappropriate benchmark for a credit derivative.

Credit recessions are non-normal long-tail distributions of events that affect credit derivative prices. Therefore, credit derivatives on corporate and sovereign bonds, during a recession or financial market stress, are illiquid and prices are more volatile than for other derivatives.

Derivative Credit Risk

Losses from loan credit risk have been much greater than derivative credit risk. For example for JP Morgan, at year-end 2015, nonperforming loans were $10.7 billion compared to total loans of $734 billion or a ratio of 1.46%. In contrast, non-performing derivative receivables of $239 million compared to total derivative receivables of $74.9 billion or a ratio 0.03%. The reason for difference was that 82%

of derivative receivable were to counterparties rated investment grade and 88% of derivatives transactions were subject to collateral agreements. (These figures are somewhat misleading. If regulators had allowed AIG to fail non-performing derivative receivables would have been several hundred millions for several money center bank.

JP Morgan uses Average Exposure ("AVG") for pricing and allocating credit capital. The Credit Valuation Adjustment (CVA) is similar to a receivables expected loss adjustment and adjusts derivative receivables for the expected loss implied by each counterparty's credit rating.

Calculating Derivative Credit and Market Risk

The key technique for evaluating derivative credit and market risk is the concept of Value at Risk (VaR). JP Morgan's Annual Report provides the best explanation of this concept.

JPMorgan Chase utilizes VaR, a statistical risk measure, to estimate the potential loss from adverse market moves in a normal market environment. The Firm has a single VaR framework used as a basis for calculating Risk Management VaR and Regulatory VaR.

The Firm employs the framework across lines of business using historical simulation based on data for the previous 12 months. The framework's approach assumes that historical changes in market values are representative of the distribution of potential outcomes in the immediate future. The Firm believes the use of Risk Management VaR provides a stable measure of VaR that closely aligns to the day-to-day risk management decision made by the lines of business, and provides the necessary and appropriate information needed to respond to risk events on a daily basis.

The Firm calculates Risk Management VaR assuming a one-day holding period and an expected tail-loss methodology that approximates a 95% confidence level.[1] VaR provides a consistent framework to measure risk profiles and levels of diversification across product types and the Firm uses it for aggregating risk across businesses and monitoring limits. Traders report these VaR results to senior management, the Board of Directors and regulators.

---

[1] Some banks use a 99% confidence level. JPMorgan, however, believes a 95% confidence level is better since the 95% probability would capture an average of 12 breaks (5% of approximately 240 trading days a year.) per year. In contrast, traders would expect a 99% probability to capture only approximately two breaks per year and, therefore, would be less effective in capturing trends in increased volatility.

Under the firm's risk management methodology, assuming current changes in market values are consistent with the historical changes used in the simulation, the firm would expect to incur VaR "band breaks," defined as losses greater than that predicted by VaR estimates, no more than five times every 100 trading days. The number of VaR band breaks observed can differ from the statistically expected number of band breaks if the current level of market volatility is materially different from the level of market volatility during the 12 months of historical data use in the VaR calculation.

Underlying the overall VaR model framework are individual VaR models that simulate historical market returns for individual products and/or risk factors. To capture material market risks as part of the Firm's risk management framework, management performs comprehensive VaR model calculations daily for businesses whose activities give rise to market risk. These VaR models are granular and incorporate numerous risk factors and inputs to simulate daily changes in market values of the historical period; traders select inputs based on the risk profile of each portfolio as sensitivities and historical time series used to generate daily market values may be different across product types or risk management systems. Management aggregates the VaR model results across all portfolios at the Firm level.

For certain products VaR does not capture specific risk parameters due to the lack of inherent liquidity and availability of appropriate historical data for these products. The Firm uses proxies to estimate the VaR for these and other products when daily time series are not available. It is likely that using an actual price-based series for these products, if available, would affect the VaR results presented.

In addition, data sources used in VaR models may not be the same as those used for financial statement valuations. In cases where market prices are not observable or where traders use proxies in VaR historical time series, the source may differ.

Since traders base VaR on historical data, it is an imperfect measure of market risk exposure and potential losses. Traders do not use it to estimate the impact of stressed market conditions or to manage any impact from potential stress events. In addition, based on their reliance on available historical data, limited time horizons and other factors, VaR measures are inherently limited in their ability to measure certain risks and to predict losses, particularly those associated with market illiquidity and sudden or severe shifts in market conditions. The Firm therefore considers other measures in addition to VaR, such as stress testing, to capture and manage its market risk positons.

Traders periodically evaluate and enhance VaR model calculations in response to changes in the composition of the Firm's portfolios, changes in market conditions, improvements in the Firm's modelling techniques and other factors. Such changes may also affect historical comparisons of VaR results. Model changes undergo a review and approval process by the Model Review Group before implementation into the operating environment.

The Firm calculates separately a daily aggregated VaR in accordance with regulatory rules ("Regulatory VaR"), which is used to derive the Firms regulatory VaR-based capital requirements under Basel III. This Regulatory VaR model framework currently assumes a ten business-day holding period and an expected tail loss methodology that approximates a 99% confidence level. Traders apply Regulatory VaR to "covered" positions as defined by Basel III, which may be different from the positions included in the Firm's Risk Management VaR. For, example, credit derivative hedges of accrual loans are included in the Firm's Risk Management VaR, while Regulatory VaR excludes these credit derivative hedges. In addition, in contrast to the Firm's Risk Management VaR, Regulatory VaR currently excludes the diversification benefit for certain VaR models."

VaR results in an income statement loss. In the past, JPMorgan has limited its average VaR to a less than 1% of estimated pretax income. (JPMorgan's pretax income for the past 5 years has averaged approximately $20 billion while average Total VaR was been limited to less than $200 million or less than 1% of its average pretax income.) In 2013, JPMorgan reduced Total Average VaR to $52 million compared to $152 million in 2012 and $101 million in 2011 because of Dodd Frank and large losses.

Diversification between products like fixed income, foreign exchange, equities, commodities etc. has historically reduced JPMorgan's VaR by over a third. These reductions indicate the economies of scale in the derivative business because historically not every commodity has been volatile at the same time.

JPMorgan does constant VaR Back testing to check VaR's accuracy. The chart in its annual report shows that for the year ended December 31, 2015, the Firm observed three VaR band breaks. Three breaks is substantially less than the 13 breaks that traders would have normally expected under a 95% confidence level for the 260 trading days in 2015. In the year ended December 31, 2015, JPMorgan posted daily Market related losses on 143 days and market related gains on 117 days.

The London Whale

In 2013, JPMorgan had a $6 billion trading loss on its credit derivatives portfolio in its Chief Investment Office (CIO). The question is how the CIO's trader, known as the London Whale, could lose $6 billion in 2013 if the total firm VaR positon was only $152 million at that time.

Between 2008 and 2011, the London Whale purchased credit derivatives of $22.9 billion to protect derivative receivables. In 2009, during the Great Recession these insurance purchases made JPMorgan $1.9 billion which offset the fact that its derivative receivables were declining in value. In 2011 and 2010, however, this insurance (the credit derivatives) became very expensive ($769 million and $403 million) as, now that the US recession was over and credit default discount rates declined, the discounted value of JP Morgan's derivative receivables increased but the value of JP Morgan's Credit Derivatives declined. Because the London Whale thought we were not going into a recession and no longer needed to hedge JP Morgan's derivative credit receivables he decided to not only offset credit derivative hedges he had on the books but to speculate and sell/insure an additional $600 billion credit derivatives to take advantage of the improving economy.

London Whale's point of view: The annual default cost of 10-year BBB credit exposure is 43 basis points or roughly .5%, or 50 basis point.

Corporate Default Risk by Rating
Average Annual Default Rates 1981-2015 (%)

Year	AAA	AA	A	BBB	BB	B	CCC/C
1	0.00	0.02	0.07	0.21	0.80	4.11	26.87
2	0.02	0.04	0.09	0.30	1.23	4.64	18.03
3	0.04	0.04	0.09	0.34	1.47	4.59	13.74
4	0.06	0.06	0.11	0.38	1.56	4.25	11.07
5	0.07	0.07	0.12	0.41	1.60	3.91	9.39
6	0.08	0.08	0.13	0.44	1.61	3.60	7.93
7	0.08	0.08	0.14	0.43	1.56	3.33	6.98
8	0.08	0.08	0.15	0.43	1.53	3.08	6.21
9	0.08	0.08	0.15	0.43	1.49	2.86	5.63
10	0.07	0.08	0.16	**0.43**	1.44	2.70	5.14

Default swaps on the 10 year CDX.NA.IG 9 index in early April 2012 were 120 basis points or 1.2%. This 10 year CDX.NA.IG 9 index Credit Default Swap included 125 equally weighted reference entities that were liquid in the Investment Grade Credit Default Swap market. This means that if you sell protection, you receive the annual coupon of 1.2%, paid quarterly over 10 years. The credit risk to your counterparty is limited because your counterparty must collateralize any gains you have on the transaction. If the past 31 years are any indication, your default costs will be 0,43% or less than 0.5%. (Assuming a recovery rate of 40% of the 0.5% after acquiring the defaulted bonds, the credit cost will only be 0.3%.) This means a spread of 0.9%. From the London Whale's point of view, U.S. corporates will improve in credit quality over the next few years. As a result, The London Whale sells, i.e. insures $600 billion in credit default swaps on U. S. corporates whose average rating is BBB+ by selling $600 billion in the CDX.NA 9 index.

JPMorgan's regulatory capital requirement is minimal (less than $100 million) since it based only on any increase in the VaR caused by the trades. JPM was selling $600 billion in credit protection in the Chief Investment Office Portfolio of owned securities which totaled approximately $400 billion i.e. a 150% increase in investment grade credit exposure.

Hedge Fund's point of view: The market for Credit Derivatives will shrink. After AIG's collapse, regulators will no longer allow insurance companies or banks to sell credit protection. After July 2012 the Volker rule will limit this activity. Credit default swaps are insurance contracts not derivatives. Credit default swaps are illiquid. Therefore, purchases of credit protection will increase in value, regardless of the health of U.S. corporates, because the markets will become less liquid.

The London Whale is naive. In the view of the hedge funds, eventually there will be more buyers of protection than sellers of protection. As the derivatives increase in value JPMorgan, as a bank, will have to mark them to market and report a market loss each quarter. The credit default swap positions were available for everyone to see because JPMorgan had to report them in its 10 Q's and 10 K's as a separate item in its Chief Investment Office's derivative reporting.

What happened – Simplified Version? JPMorgan sold $600 billion of 10-year CDX.NAIG.9 credit protection at 1.2%. When JPMorgan could no longer control the market, the credit protection cost increased to 1.3% -- a loss of .1% a year for 10 years or a total loss of approximately 1%. A 1% loss on $600 billion was $6 billion. Based on historical default experience, if JPMorgan could have held the position it would have made money on the transactions over the long term. In the short term, JPMorgan had a substantial hit to its income and its reputation. This is an example of the risk of making mark-to-market transactions as opposed to accrual transactions and is why Dodd Frank was so adamant about reducing proprietary trading.

JPMorgan reported its credit derivatives positions and profits and losses in its 9/30/11 10Q. It did not report this information in its 3/31/12 10Q. However, the 3/31/12 financial release did disclose the change in the Chief Investment Office's VaR between 12/31/11 and 3/31/12. During that three-month period, CIO VaR increased from $69 million to $129 million. Because of this, JP Morgan Average Total VaR increased from $113 million at 12/31/11 to $170 million at 3/31/12. The actual VaR at 3/31/12 was $186 million.

Conclusion: VaR works. No one could miss changes of this magnitude! The cost of closing out the positions was $6 billion.

JP Morgan response: In order to demonstrate that JPMorgan could absorb such a loss without difficulty, it made a number of extraordinary accounting adjustments. JPMorgan took a $1.0 billion gain on the CIO investments held to maturity securities portfolio. It reduced loan loss provisions by $2.1 billion. It obtained a gain of $.8 billion on the Debt Valuation Adjustment because its debt declined in value due to the reported trading loss. It recorded a $.5 expected recovery on a Bear Steams note. It lowered the prior quarters earning by $.5 billion so the quarter-to-quarter comparison showed less of a decline. In total, these accounting adjustments added $4.9 billion to earnings. As a result, three months later at 6/30/12 net earnings were down only $.4 billion to $5.0 billion versus $5.4 billion at 3/31/12.

JPMorgan did not violate the letter of the Volker Rule since the transactions occurred prior to July 2012 when the Volker rule took effect. However, JPMorgan did violate the spirit of the Volker Rule. Selling Credit Protection without offsetting purchases is clearly proprietary trading. The result was that Volker appeared to be right about derivatives. Traders who have been successful in the past tend to be more speculative in the future. Bank managements, in turn, have a tendency to mistake past luck for skill. The conclusion of the regulators from this incident was that regulators should limit proprietary trading.

Chapter 7:
Conclusion

Democracy has been called the worst form of government other than any other form of government that has been tried. Just like democracy, "capitalism is the worst form of economic system except for any other form of economic system that has been tried". Capitalism, like democracy, needs checks and balances. In a democracy, we have the congress, the courts and the President. In a capitalistic country, we need managements, accountants, auditors, boards of directors and regulators.

Just as our highly competitive democratic political system, in the long run, rewards fairness that leads to political progress, our highly competitive capitalist economic system, in the long run, rewards competence that leads to economic progress. Signs of stress in our democratic political system are demonstrations and strikes. Sign of stress in our capitalistic economic system are bankruptcies and fraud.

The word "credit" is derived from the Latin word _credere_ meaning to believe. If we are to believe in capitalism, we need responsible and fair borrowing and lending i.e. ethical borrowers and banks.

In 2008-2009, we saw the costs of unethical borrowers and banks. Borrowers borrowed who had no chance of repayment and bankers lent who were indifferent to repayment since they securitized the loans. The result for borrowers were painful defaults. The result for banks were costly losses. Fortunately, for us, what the US needed and what Congress and the Regulators provided was government bailouts and increased regulation.

Over the past decade, regulators have convicted many banks of unethical practices. Examples include money center banks that:

- created thousands of unauthorized checking accounts,
- colluded on rigging LIBOR, the London Interbank Offering Rate, to their advantage;
- opened illegal Swiss bank accounts to hide money off shore; and
- provided lax loan standards for securitized loans.

In some cases, there were not only fines, but also admissions of guilt and removal of the Bank President and or Chief Operating office.

My own experience would suggest that this regulation was appropriate. While I was Credit Officer for JP Morgan Global Markets, I encountered three incidents of impropriety and/or narrow self-interest during 1994 and 1995.

The first incident occurred concerning the development of a Global Derivative Clearing House. A Global Derivative Clearing House would have substantially reduced credit risk from derivative trading such as the type that occurred with AIG in 2008. The JP Morgan Swaps Group vetoed efforts to create a Clearing House because they thought they could make more money without a clearinghouse since other banks would ultimately have to offset their transaction with a highly rated bank like JP Morgan. It was not until 20 years later, after the crisis of 2008-2009, that regulators finally required banks to clear their derivatives though a clearinghouse or hold substantially increased capital against them.

The second incident occurred when the Swap Group falsely reduced JPMorgan's estimated future credit exposure by $16 billion on long dated forward foreign exchange forwards. Since management charged the traders bonus pool for this potential future exposure, pointing out this error was not popular with traders.

The third incident occurred when JPMorgan Securities regularly incurred excessions on almost a third of its equity trades. These trades were to mutual finds like Fidelity, who would execute a trade at 10:00 am one morning and tell the traders at 10:00 am the following morning which fund should be allocated the trade. There was no real risk to JP Morgan since Fidelity would always honor the trade, but it made it impossible to identify true errors. It was not until 5 years later that Elliot Spitzer; the Attorney general for New York sued the mutual funds (rather than the banks) for this practice and won millions of dollars. Mr. Spitzer won because the Mutual Funds in their prospectuses had stated that they would always act in the interest of their shareholders. The Funds did not want to defend themselves in court for a practice that clearly benefited the management of the funds at the expense of the shareholders. (If the trades went up, management put the trade into a new small mutual fund with higher management commissions. If the trades went down, management put the trades into a large old fund where it had little effect.) JP Morgan asked me to leave the Bank one-hour after I had disclosed this information to senior management.

In light of increased supervision by regulators, such incidents are unlikely to occur today. Regulators have fined and regulated banks to the extent that they are now substantially more sensitive to ethical responsibilities. For example, JP Morgan today has very different ethical standards than it did in 1994-1955. Their policies today as listed in their 2015 annual report under Compliance Risk Management are as follows:

The Firm has in place a Code of Conduct (the "Code"), and each employee is given annual training in respect of the Code and is required annually to affirm his or her compliance with the Code. The Code sets forth the Firm's core principles and fundamental values, including that no employee should ever sacrifice integrity - or give the impression that he or she has. The Code requires prompt reporting of any known or suspected violation of the Code, any internal Firms policy, or any law or regulation applicable to the Firm's business. It also requires the reporting of any illegal conduct, or conduct that violates the underlying principles of the Code, by any of the Firm's employees, customers, suppliers, contract workers, business partners, or agents. Specified employees are specially trained and designated as "code specialists" who act as a resource to employees on Code of Conduct matters. In addition, concerns may be reported anonymously and the Firm prohibits retaliation against employees for the good faith reporting of any actual or suspected violations of the code. The Code and the associated employee compliance program are focused on the regular assessment of certain key aspects of the Firm's culture and conduct initiatives.

Thanks to the Regulators, banks are unlikely to be repeat the behavior I faced in 1994-1995.

On the other hand, while banks, particularly investment banks will always push the boundaries of legality, regulators are bureaucratic and there is the danger of over regulation. Today, regulators have over whelmed most banks with information requirements because regulators no longer have confidence in the banks. However, information requirements alone can never adequately supervise the extremely complex activities of traders and bankers.

Therefore, like our democratic political system, our capitalistic economic system will never run perfectly and will move back and forth between too much regulation and too little regulation. Fortunately, today we have in place a uniquely qualified and competent capitalist check and balance regulatory system that makes us the envy of the rest of the world.

www.ingramcontent.com/pod-product-compliance
Lightning Source LLC
Chambersburg PA
CBHW081459070526
44586CB00019B/2427